Facts & Feelings in the Classroom

Facts & Feelings in the Classroom

LOUIS J. RUBIN

**Benjamin S. Bloom • Elliot W. Eisner
Richard M. Jones • Abraham Maslow
Edward J. Meade, Jr. • Michael Scriven
Ralph W. Tyler**

Walker and Company, New York

First published in the United States of America in 1973
by the Walker Publishing Company, Inc.

Published simultaneously in Canada by Fitzhenry &
Whiteside, Limited, Toronto.

ISBN: 0-0827-0382-8

Library of Congress Catalog Card Number: 77-186190

Printed in the United States of America.

Book designed by JAMES E. BARRY

TABLE OF CONTENTS

1.

In the course of human events all social institutions fall behind the times and threaten to become obsolete. When this occurs, change is essential; the institution must either adapt itself or go under. In the case of the schools, seemingly, the time for radical reform is at hand.

chapter 1
SCHOOLING
AND LIFE
.
Louis J. Rubin

THE CHILD SETTING OFF on his first day of school embarks upon an experience that is a good deal more critical than he, or perhaps even his parents, suspect. In the course of his schooling—compelled by law for at least a decade—he will come to a lasting image of himself and a sense of the way he fits into his world. When the experience has concluded, it is almost a certainty that the memories stored in his psychic attic will continue to exert profound influence for the remainder of his life. Our school encounters are a powerful force in shaping the kinds of persons we think ourselves to be and in molding the underpinnings of the life choices we ultimately will make. Apart from the family circle, no other environment has a greater impact upon the child's conception of himself and his view of the social scenes in which he is involved.

George Orwell's vision of what is now a not-too-distant future is a vision of a society with great knowledge and technology but humanly bankrupt. It remains an ominous warning of what may yet come. Man has great destructive powers, and his current civilization may perish with a bomb or an environment that has been deprived of its hospitality. More-over, Orwell did not foresee another side of the prob-lem—that man's needs for survival go beyond the material. Silvan S. Tomkins, for example, notes:

> It now appears that there are primary *biologi-cal* motives *other* than the drives of hunger, thirst, air, and sex. There are the primary *affects* or feelings—of surprise, interest, enjoyment, distress, fear, anger, shame, and contempt.[1]

So even Orwell's dehumanized society may not be a viable option. The contemporary plagues of violence, apathy, drugs, suicide, and crime—to speak of the more notable of our social ills—are a grim reminder that many people do not find their lot in life ade-quate. The hard lesson of our time is that knowledge is not enough.

Throughout their history our schools have directed their efforts toward the cognitive development of their students. Sterling M. McMurrin describes such edu-cation as follows:

> The cognitive function of instruction is directed to the achievement and communication of knowl-edge, both the factual knowledge of the sciences and the formal relationships of logic and mathe-matics—knowledge as both specific data and generalized structure. It is discipline in the ways of knowing, involving perception, the inductive, deductive, and intuitive processes, and the tech-niques of analysis and generalization. It involves both the immediate grasp of sensory objects and

---

1. Silvan S. Tomkins, in Foreword to *Daydreaming—An Introduc-tion to the Experimental Study of Inner Experience,* by Jerome L. Singer (New York: Random House, 1966).

the abstractive processes by which the intellect
constructs its ideas and fashions its ideals. . . .[2]

In contrast, the *affective* function of instruction, as
he explains it for us, involves a different set of concerns; it

. . . pertains to the practical life—to the emotions, the passions, the dispositions, the motives, the moral and aesthetic sensibilities, the capacity for feeling, concern, attachment or detachment, sympathy, empathy, and appreciation.[3]

The emphasis on cognition has had impressive results—notably, in producing some extraordinarily knowledgeable graduates. But the scant concern for affect has worked its own havoc, breeding a sizable number of unhappy people. Too rarely has the student been helped to deal, on a personal level, with the problems of human behavior—his and others'. Worse, much of the educational process has seemed out of touch with his life.

This irrelevancy finds its roots in what might be called curricular obsolescence. Often the *materials* that are used to present subject matter are out of keeping with the experiences of the student—the use in urban ghettos of middle-class folklore, depicting sterilized and unreal nonadventures in suburbia, serves as an example. Moreover, as Elliot W. Eisner demonstrates in a later chapter, the *methods* of instruction have been designed to a great extent for the kinds of children who can comfortably acquire knowledge through verbal, abstract processes—thus

2. Sterling M. McMurrin, "What Tasks for the Schools?"
        Saturday Review, 14 January 1967, p. 41.
3. Ibid.

handicapping the many youngsters whose preferred learning style is nonverbal and nonabstract. In other words, the ways in which children are taught have in some cases made formal learning seem impossible to them. But above all, much of the instruction has ignored the student's feelings, particularly those feelings that for him are persistent and overriding. These emotions, centering on the central issues of identity and relationship to the external world, define, more than anything else, what is meaningful and meaningless for the student.

The dominant theme of this volume, then, is that an abiding concern for affect must become a fundamental part of the curriculum—and that many aspects of the child's emotional life can be fused with his cognitive learning. While the argument seems obvious, its simplicity is deceptive for the secondary implications reach deep into our conceptions of the educational process and our basic notions as to what schools are for. These implications, it seems to me, lead to at least six premises, each of which demands a substantial departure from prevailing convention. To wit:

(1) Our behavior is influenced by both our thoughts and our feelings. So far as our actions are concerned, therefore, reason and emotion are of a piece.

Accordingly, since schools are interested in the shaping of behavior, (2) children's feelings are a useful basis for instruction. In pursuing such instruction, however, it is imperative that thought (cognition) and emotion (affect) be integrated so that one informs the other.

And, in pursuing such instruction, (3) we well may find it necessary to revise our ideas regarding the purpose of education.

For whatever other outcomes are achieved, (4) schooling should be a constructive rather than destructive experience.

Hence, (5) the quality of school life must itself be made more sanative, more health inducing.

This, in turn, (6) will require an approach to teaching and learning that is different from that which now goes on.

To expand upon these implications, it is apparent at the outset that there is no way to separate a child's education from his emotional life—whether we should so desire or not. *Reason and emotion are of a piece.* More or less fixed feelings about people and objects—organized into larger frameworks of attitudes, values and beliefs—place us in our universe, give meaning and substance to our lives, and filter our perceptions of reality. For better or worse, we are complex creatures who, in seeking to satisfy our urges, are driven in part by our reason and knowledge, and in part by our passions, anxieties, and our convictions as to what in life is important and unimportant.

The child who feigns illness or erupts into temper tantrums to avoid going to school, the compulsive A student, the rebellious dropout—all manifest this interrelationship. Children are not exempt from the condition of humanness; and when we treat them as if they were, confusion, misunderstanding, and worse are the result.

We are still at the frontier of understanding man's nature in its total complexity, but our studies of behavior and learning suggest that our sights are too short when we seek to deal with a child's education on the basis of reason alone. It may be, therefore, that perhaps our greatest sin in schooling has been to place emotion outside the organized program of instruction. It is in fact a redundancy to argue that the curriculum should include the child's affective life—it *is* included, whether we wish it so or not. How else can we explain the bright lad who reads poorly, the girl who deliberately turns in wrong answers to examination questions, and the third-grader who has already been taught that he is an educational incompetent?

It is perhaps ironic that, once the need for conjoining thought and feeling is acknowledged, it appears that the alliance can improve not only the student's intellectual achievement, but also his emotional growth as well. As Richard M. Jones argues so persuasively later in this volume: *children's feelings are a useful basis for instruction.*

The force of the coalescence can be more clearly understood when we consider the impact of feeling on motivation, cognition, and behavior—three of education's most primary concerns. Affect, in essence, is inextricably linked with those powerful human variables that make—or break—individual growth. And while the linkages involve a constantly shifting organic mix of these factors, the threads of the pattern are somewhat discernible.

AFFECT AND MOTIVATION

Why, the novice teacher is oft moved to ask, do children not try harder to learn? The subject matter, to be sure, may have a dreariness that dissipates the spirit, but more often than not the child sees little connection between the events of the classroom and his own real world. It is our habit, in schools, to counteract this diffidence with motivational bribes of one sort or another. We may offer a gold-sealed diploma in return for high grades or threaten college rejection as a consequence of low ones. We try, in short, to appeal to one or more of the child's needs. Our biological needs, more easily understood, operate primarily on the basis of deficiency—when we are hungry we look for food; when cold, for warmth; and so on. Motivation through affect, though less obvious, is an equally potent incentive in humans. The process of socialization, for example, combines both negative sanctions (avoidance of distress, fear, shame and contempt) and positive reinforcements (enjoyment, interest, pleasure, success, and so on). It may be that in seeking to appeal to the learner's sense of need, we have misread the signs and offered counterfeit tokens as a substitute for true emotional satisfaction. It may also be that in the case of many children, we have created permanent damage through an excessive use of aversive and punitive reinforcements.

There is reason to believe, for example, that anxiety, fear, and the threat of failure—in dosages too large to be borne comfortably—may preclude successful learning for many of our students. Even high-achieving students often excel at the cost of permanent insecurity and anxiety. Many seemingly successful adults still have bad dreams about being ill-prepared for an examination, or of receiving a low grade. Anxiety of this sort is a useless and painful burden that can be extraordinarily difficult to shed. The ultimate toll of the burden is a defective self-concept, causing us to depend upon external figures for indications of our correctness and our worth. Internalized self-esteem comes hard in this setting.

The constructive use, rather than suppression, of individuality and emotion provides a bulwark against the pressure and anxiety that the traditional competitiveness of the school may otherwise engender. The requisites of a healthy relationship between emotion and motivation are two: that feelings be recognized and dealt with therapeutically; and that, to the largest extent possible, motivation be direct and internalized. Respecting the concerns of children, in effect, decontaminates the cognitive task and prevents bad emotion from interfering with the acquisition of knowledge.

It is only after the child is protected from excessive emotional stress that authentic motivation can be invoked. I believe that Jones is right when he contends that some emotional discomfort is essential. There is, however, a fine line between what is necessary and what is too much, and the odds are that we have been more often guilty of excess than we suspect. In the case of some compensatory programs for socially abused children, and in misinterpretations of the open school, for example, we have tended to confuse permissiveness and overindulgence with freedom. Once the learner's true emotional needs have been identified, whether these are a matter of autonomy or constraint, authentic motivation—incentive spawned by a sense of potency and a desire to use one's capabilities—can be set in motion. As Richard DeCharms points out, this is something quite different from achievement that is induced by external rewards:

> We are suggesting that the crux of the distinction between extrinsic and intrinsic motivation may be in the knowledge of feeling or personal causation. The satisfaction deriving from the experience of personal causation is the satisfaction of having accomplished something by individual effort. The satisfaction of possession of objective rewards or results of effort must be distinguished from the above.[4]

4. Richard DeCharms, *Personal Causation* (New York: Academic Press, 1968), p. 328.

The behavior produced by intrinsic motivation is quite unlike that which stems from stress, anxiety, or the desire for a material reward. The difference is precisely that which exists between the man who gardens for pleasure and the one who does so for a salary. Self-motivated people are variable, plastic, adaptive, and characterized by seemingly endless energy for the activities they choose to engage themselves in. In contrast, externally motivated individuals seem to be somewhat more fixed and rigid, less capable of extracting satisfaction from their labor, more susceptible to fatigue, and driven, chiefly, by the anticipation of a wanted something that will come later; in short, they engage in a trade—exchanging drudgery for a substantive payoff. They are diminished by the absence of two vital qualities: control and freedom. They have no choice but to defer, pawnlike, to the constraining conditions that regulate the reward they seek.

Later in the book, in his chapter on mastery learning, Benjamin S. Bloom makes it clear that such motivation *can* be provided and—of even greater significance—that its existence generates substantial benefits in the way of cognitive achievement. Thus, a double victory may be possible: by devoting greater attention to the student's emotional well-being, we may create both a more contented human being, and at the same time one who learns more efficiently. In view of these circumstances, there seems little reason for not rejecting, once and for all, the ancient myth that a harsh tutor is necessary if good education is to go on. Despite its desirability, however, achieving a sound balance between reason and emotion will be anything but easy.

Amid all that is unclear about affect, the available research evidence suggests that it is heavily influenced by two factors: by the individual's internal drive and by the external stimuli in his environment. What this means, obviously, is that our efforts at individualization must go far beyond intelligence. Children differ, not only in their mental abilities, but in their drives, their attitudes, their ability to withstand tension, and—importantly—in the ways they feel about themselves. True individualization, therefore, requires that we discover whatever we can about a child's emotional characteristics, and plan his educational experiences accordingly.

AFFECT AND BEHAVIOR

The child who has memorized the Ten Commandments may not be compelled to follow them. Knowledge alone does not guarantee specified behavior. In teaching, we may separate feeling and thought in order to deal with one or the other somewhat more precisely. But unless they are once again conjoined—somewhere in the instructional process—school is unlikely to have much effect on the ways in which children respond to their life situations. The present educational system, concentrating as it does on the immediate goals, may—if education is preparation for life—be missing the point.

Man's behavior is largely determined by his attitudes, beliefs, values, and perceptions; these, for the most part, are outside the curricular pale. In the whole of the curriculum, for example, there is little relief for the child who frets about his size, for the one who questions his talents or despises the color of his skin, or for the one who has no sense of identity. Children faced with these difficulties can only view the dates of the French and Indian wars as inconsequential. Admittedly, as a public institution, there are limits regarding the extent to which the school can intervene in the "private" lives of its clients. Moreover, our lack of expertness in dealing with matters of human emotion makes such education tricky ground at best; but we cannot explain the world to children—nor to ourselves, for that matter —if we do not deal with the noncognitive processes that control our thoughts and actions. Given sufficient incentive, we can acquire greater expertness and come closer—if only elliptically—to the concerns of our students.

It has now become unmistakably evident that if we do not address ourselves to these concerns, we may well fail the students we serve. The critical problem resides in what has popularly been called the generation gap. Reduced to its essence, we have assumed that certain attitudes, beliefs, and values are universal, and that it is the responsibility of the school to inculcate these in young people. The events of the past decade, however, have demonstrated that these attitudes, beliefs, and values are *not* universal, and that the young prefer to fashion their own value system rather than to inherit a second-hand package.

Where values are concerned, the individual always has a choice—one may opt to be selfish or caring, to strive for affluence or inner harmony. Moreover, when societal instability and discontinuity occur, what we regard as the conventional value system must inevitably change. Whereas, for example, substantial amounts of leisure time were once a luxury, uncommitted time has now become a problem for many Americans. It is not surprising, therefore, that what we regard as youthful alienation is more than mere rebellion and a rejection of authority—it is a bid for a different way of life.

The various counter-cultures that have arisen of

late serve as a ready illustration. Among the present younger generation there is a strongly vested interest in a kind of cult of individuality. For many of the young, consequently, there seems little reason to respect the rules of the establishment—and even less to join it. The result of this rejection is that a classic incentive—successful participation in the mainstream of the social organization—no longer exists. Schools are now hard pressed to influence, much less inspire, the life aspirations of their clients; for what is now of primary importance, at least for the alienated group, is to become self-directive and to own one's emotional soul. For these students, school—if it is to be meaningful—must allow one to participate in determining the course of his own academic and spiritual growth.

As a result of our reluctance to allow young people to examine alternative beliefs and values, a near tragedy has come to pass—the tendency on the part of young people to deny the credibility of education. It need not have happened. With a greater emphasis on children's emotional concerns, on process rather than product, and a lesser emphasis on transmitting a "ready-made" morality, we might have helped, rather than hindered, the young in their search for meaning and personal worth in a time of social transition.

AFFECT AND COGNITION

That feelings condition cognitive thought is well-known. We accept, and sometimes search for, misperceptions that fulfill our emotional needs. Similarly, we do not always think rationally, preferring instead irrationalities that somehow decrease our emotional tensions. It is difficult to catch ourselves at sloppy thinking, simply because the distortions are, in one way or another, frequently satisfying. It seems reasonable to argue, hence, that what we can learn and what we cannot learn or forget are heavily influenced by our feelings.

The point—as Jones demonstrates later—is that feelings can *aid* or *hinder* the cognitive process. Properly taken into account, they can make a subject more interesting, learning more easy, motivation more personalized, and behavior more productive. *It is imperative that thought (cognition) and emotion (affect) be integrated so that one informs the other.*

Because affect is central to motivation, and because all behavior is motivated, there is a natural linkage upon which we can draw. But, it must be remembered as well, that feelings also influence the intensity of our motivation. We may, for example, be inclined to do what is kind or fair, and we may *know* of situations in which we can act out these inclinations—we can donate money to charity, work to organize voters, give time to a public service organization, help disadvantaged children, and so on. The inclination to act in a particular way at a particular time, however, is heavily dependent upon the feeling we attach to what we perceive. The impulse to act, in sum, arises not from inert knowledge but from the motivation set loose by the emotional counterparts of the knowledge.

Children's perceptions, and the emotions they attach to these perceptions, once recognized by the teacher, can be used with telling effect to better understand the child and to invent learning activities that facilitate cognitive growth, that enhance emotional stability, and that strike at the very heart of what the child considers relevant.

Abstract, rational thought, in its unadulterated state, is not a natural way for most children to deal

with their universe—the value of abstract reason is not
grasped unless the child feels that it somehow has a
bearing on his existence. Consequently, unless cognition is related in some effective way to the student's
reality—to his life—it is likely that it will not be
applied, or perhaps not even learned. For example, in
one of our studies, we discovered a nine-year-old
black girl who had failed the third grade—among
other things, she was unable to "get" the concept of
division. Yet she could reel off the complicated kin-
ship system of her large, extended family with an
ease that would be difficult for an anthropologist! In
the same vein, most adults have forgotten the cognitive lessons they attained with such difficulty throughout their years of schooling, but retained the psychological by-products that most closely touched their
lives.

All of this is to say that what is real, what is experiential, what is of concern to the child, is half-
learned already. John Dewey describes this as follows:

> To "learn from experience" is to make a back-
> ward and forward connection between what we
> do to things and what we enjoy or suffer from
> things in consequence. Under such conditions,
> doing becomes a trying; an experiment with the
> world to find out what it is like; the undergoing
> becomes instruction—discovery of the connec-
> tion of things. . . . Experience is primarily an
> active-passive affair; it is not primarily cogni-
> tive.[5]

We need to expend more effort in finding the
strongest connective tissue between life in the school

5. John Dewey, *Democracy and Education* (New York: Macmillan,
1964), p. 140.

and life outside. There is no reason why the interests of children—both cognitive and emotional—cannot be reflected in what they are required to do in school. And, of even greater moment, there also is no reason why the cognitive lessons we wish children to learn cannot be brought to bear upon their affective concerns, or the reverse. All of which is to say that feelings and facts can be joined together in a mutual alliance.

It would be well to observe, at this point, that in a healthy curriculum there is a simultaneous interplay between cognition and affect. If they are treated as separate entities, so that the child is scheduled to think cognitively at nine o'clock during arithmetic, and to explore his affective inclinations at ten o'clock during the music period, the goal we seek will elude us. Similarly, games, sociodramas, and simulations that trigger emotional feelings are meaningless exercises if they are not connected with some sort of cognitive learning. One finds, here and there, well-intentioned teachers who sometimes ask their students to act out feelings of, say, aggression or frustration. In the same spirit, other teachers ask their students to "explore" one another's faces with their hands, in order to "deepen their sensory awareness." These somewhat exotic excursions into the emotional terrain—because of their artificiality and their disconnection with the learner's actual life experiences—are of questionable value. Under special circumstances they may have some utility, but they are difficult to use properly, posing special pitfalls of their own; and in many cases they go well beyond the legitimate business of the school.

The point here is that by adding an affective dimension to the present, cognitively oriented curriculum—if managed with sensitive skill—we can

enhance learning, infuse schooling with a new kind
of life and zest, improve motivation, and greatly
enrich the academic ideas under study. Conversely,
by bringing children's authentic feelings into the
open and by making them a basis for cognitive exploration and understanding, we can help the student
to deal with the pervasive and overriding concerns
with which he must now struggle on his own—his
emotional liabilities and the attitudes of mind that
undermine his behavior.

The line that separates the individual's private life
from those matters that are proper for a compulsory school is exceedingly delicate. We have no right,
in short, to compel children to deal with their feelings
in public. When, however, in the course of a scholarly
and academic discussion, the individual's emotional
response *to the ideas at stake* are brought into play,
there is a legitimate and defensible relevance. Moreover, when these feelings bend naturally toward such
questions as How would I choose to behave in this
situation? On what feelings would I base my decisions?—questions that lie at the root of man's humanness—there is much to be gained; for a curriculum
that never addresses itself to these questions is hiding
its head in intellectual sand.

In its highest form, learning is holistic and organic.
Encouraging emotionality at the expense of logic, or
rationality at the expense of feeling, results either in
the subjugation of man to the tyranny of his passions,
or in raw intellectualism. In both instances we achieve
but half a person. What is more, the child is not de-
ceived when the textbook or teacher preaches one lesson and the school setting itself preaches quite another. Children learn much in their school lives that
does not appear in the course of study. Thus: *the quality of school life must itself be made more sanative,*

more health inducing.

Preoccupied with how much children learn, with the logic of reason and the rationality of fact, we have produced schools that, in the cases of many children, have achieved impressive, even awesome, heights of scholarship. But the emotional toll, the psychological scar tissue, which in many instances has had a profound debilitating effect on the child, seems largely to have gone uncorrected. We cannot, therefore, lightly dismiss the indictments—set forth by John Holt, Charles Silberman, Ivan Illich, and others—that schools sometimes dehumanize, brutalize, and otherwise impair the child's psychological well-being. It should not be so. *Schooling should be a constructive rather than destructive experience.* One need not suffer in order to become knowledgeable; a happy school need not be an educational wasteland, and tedium need not be confused with rigor. There is a common human tendency to believe that whatever is difficult is valuable, a tendency that is particularly pronounced in schooling. Some parents worry if their children happen to like school. While the young should adapt to at least a minimal amount of structure, and while order and organization are essential, it is not necessary that the child's spirit be maligned, or that his creativity be quelled, or that he be kept captive in a joyless environment. If things went right, children would feel deprived—not delighted—when school was out. It is therefore the very quality of the school environment itself that must be reexamined and made more salutary.

It is essential, in this reexamination, that we avoid a temptation to defend the status quo, that we deal with wholes rather than fragments, and that we seek to anticipate the future rather than mirror the past. The history of school reform has a piecemeal, tinker-

ing quality that has consistently diminished the usefulness of innovations. Because the reforms must
involve the overall environment, it is imperative that
we take a hard look at the entire range of school experience—both the explicit and implicit dimensions
of curricula, and both the extrinsic and intrinsic
kinds of learning referred to by Abraham Maslow a
bit later. The historical record of educational change,
particularly during the past decade, is somewhat dis-
mal in that it too often has come to little more than a
pastiche. The current movements for "free schools"
and for informal education, as cases in point, have
great potential. They are very likely to fail, however,
if they are superimposed upon the rationale that un-
derlies the present school. Both movements were conceived out of a different conception of educational
purpose, and they cannot be used willy-nilly, any
more than a contemporary lamp can be placed, with
pleasing effect, upon a colonial table.

   In the time ahead, if the reconstruction of education
is to have any lasting vitality, the reforms must be
based foursquare upon the egregious problems that
are described in the chapters that follow. We must
acknowledge, for example, that a quality education
for all youth cannot be achieved through a universal
solution, and that our present schools are inappropriate for many of our children. And, of greatest importance, we must look anew at the fundamental
postulation that true learning is experiential.

   If true learning in the explicit curriculum is experiential, then the corollary for our implicit curriculum can be said to be: *what is experienced is learned.*
For many of our students, this experience has left
something to be desired. Like all institutions, the
poorest of our schools have over time developed their
own inertia, their own bureaucratic impedimenta, and

their own *raison d'etre*. In these circumstances the student has little choice but to endure matters as best he can.

There are, to be sure, great schools and gifted teachers to be found here and there. In the main, however, it seems fair to argue that the growing alienation of the young toward schooling is not without its cause. Students often find, as a case in point, that creativity and independence are largely unrewarded and sometimes dangerous. If they rebel, if they demonstrate strong feeling or the desire to control their own condition, they are exhorted to be obedient, well-behaved, unquestioning of authority, and resigned to the system.

There is also, of course, another side to the coin. In an age of dissent and protest, it is hardly surprising that many of the young have seen fit to rebel, not to overcome any real trangressions, but rather for the sheer joy of the sport. Once again, then, it is difficult to generalize and essential to understand both the rules of the game and the intent of the players. Where —by design or by error—we have taught our students to be massive conformists or alienated rebels, to distrust school and society alike, and to mistrust their own experience, a vast number of correctives are in order. And where the young are merely experimenting with the more fascinating maneuvers of some of their elders, the call, as always, is for tolerance and patience.

What is most to be regretted in the confusion of the times is that, uncertain of our ground, we too often ebb and flow between extremes. In some schools the student is expected to recall data, howsoever meaningless, with machine-like precision, and in others, to plot his own educational growth without benefit of adult guidance.

Finally, in our reexamination of the school environment, we must also look again at our *methods* of teaching—for herein is contained still another "hidden" curriculum, experienced and learned by the student. The cognitive skills at which instruction is aimed, for example, are basically twofold: skills relating to factual information—knowing and manipulating data within a formal structure (as in mathematics and logic); and skills having to do with the *process* of knowing—induction, deduction, generalization, and so on. In the traditional curriculum, these latter skills—processes of knowing—in many cases have been treated in a manner that frustrates and mystifies. For the student has been taught the devices through which we know, but has been denied their use and exploration except along narrowly confined lines. Thus the implicit curriculum of Truths and Right Answers is put in direct conflict with the explicit curriculum, which presumes a trust in, and a continuous experiencing of, the process of knowing. It would, of course, be senseless to require that *all* learning be experiential—some Truths and Right Answers must be taught, as this is at times most efficient and expedient. But a healthy balance must be struck between heuristics and pedantry.

Not infrequently, the very subject of instruction itself is subverted through such mystification. In civics classes, for example, "democracy" is sometimes preached in a rigidly controlled atmosphere to captive subjects. Since the essence of "democracy," like many other moral values, cannot be understood unless it is experienced, the result of such teaching predictably takes one of two forms: passive acceptance or active rejection.

We are all familiar with the message, Do as I say, not as I do. This in itself is confusing to a child. But a much greater problem arises when the message is, Don't do as I say. Most adults have difficulty coping with double-edged messages—especially when one set of expectations is explicit and the other either hidden, or conveyed and then denied. To a child who wishes to please, conflicting expectations create massive confusion and frustration.

The contradictions in the expectations schools impose upon their students range from opposing demands ("Use your own imagination" and "The form we always use is") to a denial of the student's actual feelings ("You *couldn't* have felt that way about it") to an outright rejection of real events that are readily apparent ("The faculty does not interfere with the student government"). Apart from the fact that an environment of contradiction is somewhat pathology-producing, these inconsistencies serve to diminish the student's confidence in the school's integrity, and to make him regard it as more of an enemy than an ally. It is commonly assumed that, in the rearing of children, such manipulations are necessary, and that once adulthood is reached, their victims are forgiving. The present generation is a bright lot, however, with a ready eye for ideological gaps, and once the conflicting messages have been sorted out, their embitterment with the system extends even further.

As we attempt to reconstruct our educational philosophy, we must of necessity deal with some larger problems. As Eisner and Meade argue later on, the greatest of these is that *we must look anew at the purpose of education and consider an approach to teaching and learning that is different from that which now goes on.* Perhaps school is not, after all, a place in which to prepare future plumbers, surgeons, and poets. Ralph W. Tyler, in his chapter, demonstrates that the weeding out of nonintellectuals, formerly an implied function of the schools, is no longer legitimate in today's society. It is my belief—certainly one that is not held alone—that the proper function of schooling ought to be that of making human beings better.

It may be, in other words, that it is more desirable to have a school in which a child learns to know himself and his world, than to have a school in which a child learns to earn a living. We are coming to see that a secure income or vocational success do not guarantee human satisfaction—we need only to look at a cross section of the citizenry to discover vast numbers of people who are vocational successes and human failures. Moreover, it may be—as some of us suspect—that the technical knowledge essential to the practice of, say, surgery or welding, is far less than we have assumed. Should this be the case, we are obliged to give serious consideration to a curriculum that has, as its predominant goal, the objective of helping the child to become a person. Later, perhaps on the job or perhaps in another sort of school, a person may learn to become a dentist or an electrician.

The notion that public education ought to serve the society's changing needs is hardly without precedent. The crisis is currently enlarged, however, for social change is occurring at an unprecedented rate. Life in America is in flux. On all sides, the signs of cultural stress and of consequent malaise manifest themselves; the inexorable trend of civilization, in sum, may have added a new emergency to an old problem, which before could be dealt with in more leisurely fashion. If it is not possible to have a school for all seasons, and if schools must be responsive to the critical problems in the social milieu, the present purposes of the educational system appear to be in desperate need of revision.

Probably the greatest difficulty we now face both in education and in the larger social system lies in the conflicting value systems that now characterize our culture. From the conclusions that can be drawn from our current youth revolt, persuading the adult society to rethink its values is both necessary and hard—and will not be easily accomplished. Because values in large measure give meaning and form to our lives, altering these values imposes a period of insecurity and stress—a price that will appear too high to those who see no benefit in change. To persuade a successful dentist that it may not be important for his son to attend college, thus violating some of the basic premises upon which the father has based his life, is an ambitious and perhaps hopeless mission. Nonetheless, the social signs about us suggest that this may indeed be precisely what must be attempted.

We cannot in good conscience dismiss the warnings of the social scientists. Our current middle-class dispositions, for example, are based upon social phenomena that, though present a hundred or more years ago, no longer exist. Those of us who learned this ancient value structure early in our lives are bound in its grasp, perhaps permanently. Yet, there now is good reason to believe that children should not necessarily inherit all of their parents' values.

It is folly to assume that our parents' or our own values will have validity for our children or for succeeding generations to come. Both attitudes toward life and life styles themselves often are perishable commodities. What was known as the frontier spirit, for example, once a cherished aspect of the American value structure, seems anachronistic in today's increasingly hedonistic society. Whereas earlier generations accepted the notion that the delay of gratification was sometimes necessary, the present one is a good deal less patient. Similarly, the old ethic of hard work—a hallowed value of times past—is less and less culturally reinforced in our time. It is also becoming apparent, moreover, that America will never have a single ethos: The great "melting pot" myth has been dispelled by the conflicting and tenaciously-held values of minority groups, who have examined—and rejected—the offers of either assimilation or unity. The peculiar paradox, then, is that effective social change is impeded on both sides of the fence; depending upon their nature, some values create problems because of their perishability and others because of their incorruptibility.

Old values perish slowly, but we must persist if we are to survive. More and more it grows evident that education's task is to prepare future citizens to make hard choices, to fashion changing values when necessary, and to solve new problems as—inevitably —they emerge.

We have, for too long now, ignored education's underside and looked away as weaknesses began to show. These weaknesses have grown to the point where they no longer can be ignored. The present system, adequate in its day, is now infirm. If obsolescence occurs when human requirements change, the reconstruction of the educational system is long overdue. Should we not begin?

editor's comments

WHILE IT MAY seem unusual to offer a commentary upon one's own writing, something of a postscript might be appropriate here. I have tried in this, the first of the volume's nine chapters, to introduce several themes, and to set the stage as well for the larger number of additional themes that are set forth by my distinguished colleagues.

As a whole, this volume is a plea for a major revision of the public school curriculum. Such a plea is by no means extraordinary in our present day and age. Indeed, the book is considerably less radical than many others that have appeared in the recent past. There are, however, some fundamental differences between this book and other recently published calls for change. The kinds of innovations herein described represent not theory alone, but theory that has withstood the test of hard research evidence and some empirical testing. And, as a second difference, the revisions that are suggested—though relatively dramatic in their scope—could reasonably be implemented in the immediate future. Social institutions such as the public school have their own inertia and do not lend themselves to radical overthrow. Changes seem to have the greatest success when they build, one upon the other, in progression. The magnitude of a change is constrained, in other words, by the degree of radicalness the public is willing to accept, and by the profession's ability to not merely introduce, but also sustain, a bold departure from convention.

The directions change must take have been given ample treatment by theorists, and some of these seem quite radical. In a recent book, for example, James S. Coleman has suggested that the present schools are obsolete, and that in the schools of the future the teaching of children and the imparting of knowledge must not be the primary goal.[6] I do not wish here to dispute Coleman's assertion—he may or may not be right. But I would like to point out that the revolutionary school he describes will take a very long time to accomplish on any widespread basis. Thus,

6. James S. Coleman, "Education in the Age of Computers and Mass Communications," *Computers, Communications, and the Public Interest,* ed. Martin Greenberger (Baltimore: The Johns Hopkins Press, 1971).

whatever the appropriateness of such long-range postulations about the future shape of education, there is, I believe, a pressing need for interim changes that will benefit
the children now in school.

There is one other difference between this volume and.
other, more radical, writings. Much has recently been
written about the relative advantages of free schools, open
education, computer-assisted instruction, and other innovations. There has been a tendency in these writings
toward overly simplistic solutions to education's problems. I do not mean by this to imply that the suggested
changes are necessarily undesirable; rather, I mean to
imply that it is doubtful whether any single, isolated
change will rescue us from our plight. We have therefore
attempted here a somewhat more holistic and at the same
time eclectic approach to educational change. Our focus,
therefore, while it is not necessarily superior, is deliberately broader and more inclusive in scope.

Let me turn now to a synthesis of the major arguments
in the first chapter. The dominant point has to do with the
need for a new kind of curriculum—one that involves
children's feelings. If we are interested in influencing children's behavior, we shall continue to fail so long as we
rely upon cognitive instruction alone. Cognitive knowledge is a powerful asset, and a prerequisite to much of
human action. In the present curriculum, however, we
seem to have behaved as if cognition determined behavior.
Knowledge is always a means to an ultimate end. These
ultimate ends, however, are not derived from pure
thought; instead, they are the product of reason and emotion, cast in the form of values. Hence, if the school is to
truly influence behavior, it must concern itself with the
broader range of feeling, thinking, and valuing.

We cannot accommodate these concerns within our
existing conception of educational purpose. Hence, in
the reform that must come, it is necessary to redefine both
the school's role and its function. This redefinition, in
turn, will demand major changes in teaching methods;
these must simultaneously be initiated in the pre-service

and in-service training of teachers.

Further, there are great defects in the present climate of learning. Drudgery is taken for granted, boredom is viewed as a necessary evil, our methods of motivating the learner are counterfeit, spontaneity has become something of a lost cause, and knowledge itself is packaged in a grossly unappetizing form. These, too, must command our attention as the needed reform takes place.

2.

The critical weaknesses of the existing educational system lie in its incapacity to provide all children with a quality education, and in its resistance to diversity. In the reform that must be pursued, then, these two weaknesses define the dominant goals.

chapter 2

THE AUTONOMOUS TEACHER

•

Ralph W. Tyler

OVER THE CENTURIES, the schools have been remarkably successful in adapting to changing conditions and accomplishing much of what was expected of them. Since the end of World War II, the pace of social change has greatly increased and the schools are facing major new demands, just as are other social institutions, such as the hospitals and health centers, law enforcement agencies, and the social services generally. The increasing applications of science and technology to agriculture, industry, defense, communications, and the professions themselves have so changed the life conditions and opportunities for most Americans that they anticipate improvements in their lives and ways of living that were viewed as utopian dreams at the beginning of this century.

A generation or two ago, poverty on the part of a majority of Americans was taken for granted. Only about 20 percent of the population was receiving ade-

quate health and medical services. High infant mortality and early disability and death were characteristic of the majority of families everywhere. Medical
and health services have developed tremendously
since that time; infant mortality has been sharply
reduced and longevity increased; and the services
provided by American medicine have been greatly
improved for the 20 percent to 30 percent of the population able to get them. Medical practice has been
meeting the expectations of middle-class patients
with whom the problems are largely those of finding
and destroying the organism causing the illness or
identifying and removing the malfunctioning organ,
replacing it by a mechanical substitute or a trans-
plant. These tasks have been well performed. But
now that the American public is expecting medical
and health services to be provided for everyone, physicians are discovering that many poor people do not
recover from illness merely by having a foreign organism destroyed or by removing an offending organ.
Poor people are less likely than the more affluent to
follow the hygienic regimen expected by the physician, and they are often anxiety ridden over the well-
being of their families while they are unable to work.
They frequently lack the extra physical resources
required to repair bodily deficiencies and often do
not have the confidence required for effective recu-
peration. Furthermore, the increasing number of
older people creates new health care problems.

Many doctors today are inclined to criticize themselves and their profession for their inability to meet
current health expectations, overlooking the great
strides medicine has made in meeting the demands of
the past generation. So it is with educators. Both
professions have a history of noteworthy successes.
Both need now to recognize the new problems and to

develop the practices and the institutional supports to respond to the new expectations.

SORTING FUNCTION OF SCHOOLS

Just as medical doctrines and practices were developed in terms of the structure of the then current society and the characteristics of the clientele so did educational policies and procedures. When most people were employed as unskilled laborers and only 5 percent were in professional or managerial occupations, most people could survive with little or no formal education and only a few would utilize college education in their work. Under these conditions the function of schools was to sort children, rather than to help them get an education, pushing out those who were judged least promising for further education and encouraging a few to go on.

The lockstep progress of instruction and the grading system used in schools were well suited to this sorting process. By moving the whole class at the same rate from topic to topic, pacing the movement in terms of the performance of the average students, those with more difficulty in learning would be certain to get further and further behind, and most would give up trying. This was reinforced by the grading system, which year by year gave low marks to those having difficulty, thus helping further to discourage them from going on, while assigning high marks to those who learned easily and quickly, thus encouraging them to continue their formal education year after year.

These policies and practices have existed for so long that we rarely note how sharply they differ from those of an institution devoted wholly to teaching and learning. For example, if you or I want to learn to play golf, we go to a golf pro, whose job is to teach us. We don't expect that after a few practice periods he will say, "You are getting a D in your work. I may have to hold you back if you don't improve." Instead, we expect him to say, "You are making progress on your drive, but you need to bring your full body into the swing. A little later I'll give you further practice on your putting to increase accuracy and decrease power." An institution concerned primarily with learning and teaching follows practices based on the available knowledge of how people learn, whereas our schools and colleges are only partly concerned with helping each student learn and are likely to be preoccupied with grading, classifying, and other functions.

This was appropriate for a society in an earlier stage when the positions available for the occupational, social, and political elite were few in number. Then the schools were a major means for rationing educational opportunities to conform to the social structure. It seemed sensible then to give everyone a chance to jump the hurdles and to record the results, reporting them in a way that would influence children and youth to seek further educational opportunities only as they were clearly successful in previous years. If the schools of an earlier day followed the plan of "mastery learning" outlined by Bloom (in chapter 5), in which 75 percent reach an A or B level, how could the social system absorb so many educated people? In my school days in Nebraska the public was satisfied with a school system in which more than half the children dropped out by the end of the sixth grade, only 10 percent went through high school and only 3 percent through college.

Today we have a different society. By the use of science and technology, we are producing our nation's requirements for food and fiber using only 5 percent of the labor force. Less than 5 percent is employed as nonfarm unskilled labor. Less than 40 percent of our total labor force is employed in producing and distributing material goods. More than 60 percent is furnishing nonmaterial services for which there is an ever-rising demand—health services, educational services, social services of various sorts, recreational services, accounting, and administration. Young people without the competency expected of one who has completed elementary education find very few jobs available. On the other hand, employment in the fields where demand is increasing requires more than high school education. Now, we need to educate all our children, but our system is geared to educate only a part. We must learn to reach children who have not been reached before, and to educate, beyond high school, youth from homes where no one has been to college before. These are new tasks for the schools, but because we have learned how to meet earlier expectations we can confidently expect that we can learn how to meet the new ones.

NEW POLICIES FOR NEW PROBLEMS

However, to solve the new problems we face, we must recognize that they demand a reexamination of present doctrines and practices to see where they require substantial reform. The notion that only more money, more teachers, and more supplies will bring the results expected is a serious mistake. We have developed our present system by both trial and error and thoughtful design. It works rather well with children from middle-class homes, homes that generally reflect the prevailing values, beliefs, habits, and practices. Now, when we seek to educate all our children we find that we are a society composed of a number of identifiably different groups with different values, habits, and practices. Southern sharecroppers are a striking example. These tenant farmers were living in a feudal society as serfs. They did not have need for the habits and skills of a modern industrial society. Goods came largely from plantation stores as advances on crop shares. Money was scarce and had limited usefulness. Protection against accident, illness, and death of parents was furnished by the extended family as part of its accepted duties. Now, agriculture in the Deep South is greatly changed, and the sharecroppers have migrated to the large cities in great numbers. Imagine the problems of families coming from this sixteenth-century background into the large American cities where they hoped to find jobs or at least food and shelter. The adults in these families had no dependable knowledge or skills to develop in their children to help them cope with many aspects of their new environment. We cannot safely assume that their learning can be fostered with the same materials and procedures used with typical middle-class children. This is only one illustration of an identifiable group in our society that requires special study in order to develop effective ways to facilitate learning.

We recognize that these are our problems as American educators because our nation is committed to the protection and development of a pluralistic society with opportunity for all, regardless of race, religion, income, or ethnic background. We cannot arrogantly take the position that the majority culture is the only acceptable one and those from without this background are not the nation's responsibility. At the time our federal Constitution was written, the ideal

of a monolithic society—such as those in Europe
from which many Americans had escaped—was
abandoned in favor of a pluralistic society in which
various religions, values, and ways of life would be
tolerated, even encouraged. But in spite of the views
thus expressed in the Constitution, many of our practices, including those in the schools, have largely assumed that our society is monolithic and that the
range of acceptable values and ways of living are
severely limited. Those not conforming to these limited patterns had few opportunities to go far in school
or to gain higher positions in occupational, social, or
political life. Now, however, that we have a more
productive society where there are more higher status
positions than can be filled by the more privileged
groups, we are able to implement in large measure
the ideals of a democratic, pluralistic society. Faced
now with the responsibility for educating all children
and for helping to raise the educational aspirations
and achievements of a majority of youth, we are discovering that teaching is complex and must employ
differentiated procedures, depending upon the background from which the children come and the environment in which they are living. It is no longer
useful to talk of "the teacher" or "the way of teaching" as though one set of qualifications or one series
of teaching methods adequately characterized effective performance in the varied conditions under
which learning must be fostered.

As we have observed learning in schools, we find
that middle-class children who have learned how to
learn before they come to school take many of the
steps in learning without requiring help from the
teacher, while children with limited experience in systematic learning need help in identifying these steps
as well as in taking them. In Bloom's essay, he em-

phasizes the requirement of sequential learning experiences in order to have mastery learning. Our interviews with schoolchildren reveal a number of cases in which children able to guide their own learning have constructed their own sequences for learning in units or topics in which neither the teacher nor the writer of instructional materials had consciously planned a sequence. But children who are not accustomed to building their own order out of unordered experiences are commonly overwhelmed by a mixture of simple and complex skills, basic ideas and illustrative examples, and prescriptive rules and principles that explain them. They require a planned sequence to enable them to move on step-by-step in their learning.

We find, too, that children who have learned how to learn are usually able to figure out for themselves as they work on school assignments what the objectives are, that is, what they are expected to learn from carrying out the assignment. On the other hand, many children appear to have no idea of what they are expected to learn and thus do not focus their attention on the desired outcome. When in doubt about the purpose of an assignment, they try to memorize the material assigned rather than to seek to analyze it, apply it to problems, compare and contrast it with other points of view, and the like.

Because many middle-class students learn what is expected without having explained to them what they are to learn, many teachers have not recognized that for some children to be able to succeed in their schoolwork, the teacher or someone else will need to serve as a role model, a live illustration of what it is that the children are expected to become. Again, we understand this in the learning of sports. If we are to guide our efforts in learning golf, we must see someone playing golf. If we are to practice making a long drive, we are greatly aided by observing someone making a long drive. So as teachers, we should realize that the children need to observe examples of the kind of behavior they are expected to learn.

Another illustration of teaching procedures that are differentiated for different children is the procedures involved in reinforcement and feedback as students practice the behavior they are trying to learn. Each successful practice effort should be rewarding to the child, and he is aided by getting some report on his unsuccessful efforts so as to know what he can do to improve. Unfortunately, our common school practice has been to give a higher grade or reward to those who already know or can do and to discourage those needing help by awarding a lower grade. Few efforts are devoted to helping the student correct unsuccessful behavior. Thus the students needing help in learning are not likely to receive much assistance.

Thus far, the illustrations of the need for new policies and procedures to meet the new problems schools are now facing have been those arising from the expectation that all children from many different backgrounds will gain a basic education and that many more than in the past will be going beyond high school graduation. There is also need for new practices that will be appropriate for the several new educational objectives schools are expected to attain. Meade suggests several in his chapter—learning to deal with confrontations constructively; learning to analyze pressing issues in terms of values involved that are worthy of respect; learning to formulate alternative courses of action in social situations and to appraise the probable consequences of each of them; and learning to make decisions in harmony with accepted values and the consequences of the actions proposed. The behavior students need to learn in order to attain these objectives is not well understood by most of us, and we have even less experience in implementing such teaching. It is clear that effective teaching requires many of us to learn new things and involves different policies and procedures for different situations. Most of us need to learn a great deal more in order to perform effectively the teaching-learning tasks that we are now facing.

CONTINUING EDUCATION OF TEACHERS

The preceding is background for understanding that teachers, as well as the members of all other professions today, must be involved in continuing education in order to achieve our collective expectations. The desirability of in-service education of teachers continuing throughout their professional careers has long been accepted both in theory and in practice, but most in-service education has not been focused either on the need for new professional competencies in given school situations or on the individual teacher's interests, needs, or goals. The requirement that teachers must earn a certain number of hours of advanced credit for advancement on the salary schedules furnished a general reward to motivate continuing education, and the usual stipulation that the courses that meet these requirements must be approved by the school system gave a nominal basis for concentrating the efforts on the acquisition of knowledge and skills needed to conduct the school's programs but, in fact, most continuing education activities have had little focus. They have been widely scattered, shotgun programs rather than carefully aimed rifle shots. A different approach is necessary.

In constructing and developing an effective and efficient program for the continuing education of teachers, consideration should be given both to the needs of the school and the needs and goals of the individual teacher. We can gain some perspective in noting the way in which other large organizations plan their in-service programs. One with which I am familiar is the U.S. Air Force. This organization bases its in-service education planning on the problems it is facing that require new competencies from some of its personnel.

A dramatic example arose in 1953 when intercontinental ballistic missiles began to be deployed. There are so many objects in the air and the immediate space beyond—some sixteen thousand of them—that it was seemingly impossible to identify on the radar-scopes some new object, such as a missle, when it was fired into this space. The RAND Corporation was given this problem to solve and came up with a solution that involved putting the orbits of all the currently existing objects on a computer program that could be continually tracked as a giant pattern. Then, a new object could be detected because its path would be different. If the new object was not an enemy missile, its path would then be added to the existing computer program and would thus not require further individual surveillance.

Obviously, the construction of such a computer program and its continuous updating was a new and complex task. The appropriate procedures to be followed by the supporting forces were also new and complex. Hence, the training of personnel both to develop and update programs and to carry on the necessary defense actions that should be taken in the light of the information provided became an imperative in focusing the in-service education of those persons who would be involved. In this case, the sequence of steps in planning was (1) identify important problems facing the organization, (2) for each problem, work out an effective and practical solution, (3) for each solution, identify the tasks to be performed by each person involved and the competencies required to perform each task, (4) identify those in the organization who already had the competencies required, and (5) in those cases where there are fewer persons with the essential competencies than those required to conduct the program for the next several years, there is clear need for in-service education focused on helping persons to gain the knowledge, skills, and other competencies that are lacking in the organization at present.

A medical institution furnishes another example of this planning procedure. As the great medical centers have learned of ways of dealing with advanced cases of malfunctioning of the heart, through such practices as open heart surgery and transplantations, they have identified new competencies that are required of physicians, nurses, and other personnel working in intensive care units. Most medical centers have limited resources to support the continuing education of nurses and technical personnel. Hence, it is necessary to concentrate on training and education focused on the acquisition of critically important knowledge and skills that are in short supply.

Schools face problems similar to those of other large organizations. The shotgun approach to continuing education of teachers in service is an ineffectual and inefficient use of the school's resources. The schools are facing new problems, requiring new solutions where new competencies will have to be learned by the teachers involved. These new ways of working require new perceptions or attitudes, new knowledge and skills. The learning of these takes time, effort, and guidance. The school cannot expect many teachers to be able to devote the necessary time and effort and to find helpful guidance on their own. Because the effectiveness of the school in solving its problems will depend upon teachers gaining the necessary competencies, the school has a stake in encouraging and supporting in-service programs that are clearly focused on these critical things.

The suggested procedure is similar to the one outlined above. The school district should identify its critical problems. In most school systems, 70 percent to 85 percent of the children are making substantial progress in learning. In these situations, there is little need for the school to invest heavily in continuing education, but in the case of the 15 percent to 30 percent of the children having difficulty in learning, there are likely to be some serious problems. For example, in most large cities there are critical problems in the "inner city." The children having great difficulty in learning come from homes where the parents have not had much education and lack experience in modern urban centers. This is the case of those recently arrived from the Mississippi Delta, where they had been living in a very different society. The education of disadvantaged children is generally recognized today as a common problem in "inner cities" and in certain rural areas. Most schools will find at least two or three critical problems that reduce the overall effectiveness of their educational efforts.

The next step is to work out possible solutions to each problem, or, more commonly, promising strategies for attacking it. In the case of the primary education of disadvantaged children, at least two different strategies are being employed in different schools. One of these is to extend the educational efforts to include the parents and other concerned groups in the community in order to build a background of influence to support and aid the work the school is doing. The other is to devise and use a learning system that specifically provides in the school program for the conditions known to facilitate learning, including such things as clear examples of what the student is to learn, immediate feedback on the success of his efforts, immediate rewards for successful performance, ample opportunities for practice, sequential organization of learning experiences, opportunity for each student to move at a pace he is able to handle, opportunity to master each unit before proceeding to the next one.

The application of either of these strategies requires new attitudes, new understanding, and new skills on the part of many of the persons that are involved. For example, the first strategy requires principals and teachers to perceive the home and the community as partners in the education of children in subjects such as reading and the language arts, arithmetic, social studies. These subjects are commonly vi wed as the exclusive educational responsibility of tł e school. Furthermore, it demands school personrel who understand ways in which the home and community can furnish situations where children can use reading, practice more effective language, employ arithmetic, and use concepts and values of the social studies. School personnel should also know ways in which the homes and community can help to arouse in children interest and curiosity in these areas and provide time, places, and encouragement to study. Finally, this strategy requires school personnel who have the skills of observation, listening, and communicating that are necessary to work effectively with parents of disadvantaged children and others who live in low-income neighborhoods.

The strategy of devising and using a learning system that specifically provides in the school program for the conditions known to facilitate learning also requires of principals and teachers new attitudes, new understanding, and new skills. They must see the task of the school as educating all children, even the disadvantaged. They must perceive the inadequacy of school programs that result in sorting instead of universal learning. They must understand the essential conditions for learning and the varied ways in which these conditions may be met. Finally, they must develop the skills required to work with children in a "mastery type" of situation, and to manage learning systems that involve varied activities and the use of aids, student tutors, electronic technology, and the like.

It should be clear from these illustrations that the solutions to some of the critical educational problems encountered in a school require the acquisition of new attitudes, knowledge, and skills on the part of the persons involved. To acquire them, in-service education is necessary. Furthermore, to learn some of these things takes a good deal of time, effort, and guidance. Hence, an effective and efficient program must be focused on what is essential to be learned by the persons who are to be involved and must be provided with the necessary support. From this point of view, the school system that seeks to attack its serious educational problems will need to plan a major part of its program of continuing education to furnish opportunities for teachers to acquire what they will need to support the strategies adopted by the school.

A second priority for in-service education planned by the school system is to provide opportunities for the newer teachers to broaden and deepen their experience so that they will have a more adequate basis for carrying on their work as competent professionals. This is similar to in-service programs provided in medicine, in business for junior executives, and in the military services. Many of these organizations have plans that guarantee that the novice in the profession gets an opportunity to work in a variety of situations under conditions where there are mature people using modern procedures, skills, and equipment. For example, in medicine, there are approved places for internships and even more carefully selected places for residencies. Leaders in medicine recognize that there are many settings where a young physician might go and quickly get into a rut, and lower his own standards or professional competence. The approved places are judged to be places to expand the young physician's environment and to help him hold high his standards of performance. School systems need to plan for their novices in the same way.

DEVELOPING WIDELY USABLE SKILLS

A third priority confronting schools is that of furnishing opportunities for teachers to develop new skills that are widely usable. The implications for curriculum reform and the corresponding new teaching techniques—some of which are described by the writers in this volume—will require extensive provisions for teacher continuing education. Meade, for example, points out that new pedagogical skills will be necessary if teachers are to handle ideological confrontations in an open classroom. Similarly, Bloom's research, demonstrating that mastery can, under optimum conditions, be assured, also has powerful implications for the upgrading of technique. Rubin's ar-

guments regarding the importance of dealing with
emotion and the need to make the learning environment more appealing will also require the development of additional teaching skills. Moreover, the
work of other scholars has further advanced our understanding of the teaching art, with implications for
teacher professional growth. Philip Jackson* for instance, has described the impressive skills of some
teachers in stimulating and guiding inquiry in discussions with students that are as well aimed and
sprightly as an oral Ping-Pong game. All of these
illustrate the value of general skills that can be used
by teachers wherever in the curriculum they are appropriate. A program for the systematic acquisition
of new techniques can thus be justifiably regarded as
a high priority. It is of great importance that such
programs be planned and supported by the school
system if desirable change is to be achieved.

AUTONOMY REQUIRES INFORMED CHOICE

The preceding discussion has dealt with the
school's needs and investment, not with the individual teacher. There is a real threat in a mass society
that the planning and operating mechanisms will lose
sight of the person, will stifle individual initiative,
and will stress conformity. On the other hand, autonomy means that an individual has a good deal of
control over his life; he has a wide range of choices;
he knows enough about the probable consequences of
each major possible course of action that he can
make an informed choice. In this sense, an autonomous person is a master of his fate, not merely

* Philip W. Jackson, *Life in the Classroom* (New York: Holt,
  Rinehart & Winston, 1968).

50 RALPH W. TYLER

buffeted about by forces outside his control and
going in directions that he has not chosen.

There is danger that a school system, as with some
other bureaucracies, will be planned and operated in
such a way that a teacher has little or no autonomy.
The only choice apparently available to him is to
submit to the pressures of the system or to sabotage
it. Fortunately, this is not a necessary characteristic,
even of a large school system. The autonomy of the
teacher can be preserved and actually augmented by
appropriate programs of continuing education.

By being one of the responsible participants in
identifying educational problems, selecting or devising strategies for their attack, identifying the new attitudes, knowledge, and skills required to carry out
the strategies, and selecting or designing possible
means for acquiring them a teacher is developing the
background for broadening his range of choices and
gaining understanding that enables him to make a
more informed choice.

The Eight-Year Study of the 1930s, a nationwide
study to show the relationship between the high
school curriculum and success in college, furnishes an
excellent illustration of the significance of teacher
participation in task forces working on curriculum
improvement. In this study, each school was given
freedom to build a curriculum that might better meet
the needs of students who were enrolling in secondary
schools because they could not find jobs during the
Depression. In spite of this freedom, many teachers
did not want to make any changes in curriculum or
instruction. It was hard for them to perceive anything
different. Some would say, "We are successful teachers. Why should we mess up what we now do well?"

Task forces consisting primarily of teachers were
established to study the problems faced by the new

kinds of students; to investigate their abilities, interests, and needs; and to obtain data on the larger social context, which had changed so markedly during the lean years. When teachers confronted these problems, they recognized the need for new strategies and also realized that they must acquire new attitudes toward youth and the role of the school, new understanding of contemporary society and youth problems, new knowledge as a basis for planning instructional units, and new skills in teaching problem solving and in participating in pupil-teacher planning. They recognized the need for workshops to afford teachers the opportunity to learn these things, and they participated in them thoughtfully and vigorously. The fact that they had a clear understanding of the serious problems on which they were working was a great help to bolster resolution and to reduce discouragement when they found that it took more effort and time than they had thought to plan and carry out the new strategies. They were no longer able to plead, "Why did we get ourselves into this hard work when we were getting along very well before?" because they knew that there were serious problems that must be solved.

In general, for a teacher to have real autonomy in working on his continuing education as a means of career development, he needs to see a larger picture than is provided by his immediate situation in order to recognize the educational problems to be solved, the opportunities for service available to him, what things he needs to learn in order to render these services, and the ways in which he can learn them. He also needs information about the rewards that will come to those who can carry on the strategies adopted by the school. By rewards, I mean the major kinds of satisfaction he can anticipate, including a sense of greater professional competence, knowledge of having aided pupils to learn important things they had not been learning, greater responsibility in the school organization, great respect and esteem from colleagues or the public. Participation in problem-solving task forces is a means by which an individual teacher can outline this larger picture and be able to make decisions about his own development with fuller understanding of the choices available to him and the probable consequences of choosing particular courses of action. In this way he is an autonomous teacher.

ALTERNATIVE WAYS OF LEARNING

Continuing education has not yet received the attention it deserves, and is, as a field, still in its developmental infancy. There are, however, some programs that provide illustrations of the variety of devices through which the autonomous teacher can learn.

Herbert Thelen and his colleagues* have devised ways by which a teacher can learn important clues from the pupils themselves. The teacher says to the children, "Will you work with me on this task? I am a dub at it. Can you show me what to do?" The realization that they can teach their teacher something often arouses great interest in children. In another study, the Center for Coordinated Education, under Louis Rubin's leadership, operated a series of projects in school districts throughout the country that demonstrated that teachers differ in their pedagogical

* Herbert A. Thelen, "A Cultural Approach to In-Service Teacher Training," in Louis J. Rubin (Ed.) *Improving In-Service Education: Proposals and Procedures for Change* (Boston: Allyn and Bacon, Inc., 1971).

strengths and weaknesses, and that a variety of inexpensive devices can make it possible for one teacher to help another—first, in identifying, and second, in acquiring teaching skills essential to the effective study of controversial issues. Reference to other aspects of teacher continuing education can also be found in the writing of Ronald Lippitt, Nathan Gage, Hilda Taba, and others.

The need for continuing professional growth has been recognized and the techniques refined in many fields other than education. Several state medical societies, for example, have surveyed their membership to identify the knowledge and skills that practitioners most desire, and have subsequently designed tape programs that the physician may play in his automobile so that he learns as he drives from place to place. The College of Dentistry at the University of Illinois has devised and distributed video tapes that provide dentists with a clear and close-up demonstration of new techniques; these dentists can also ask questions and clarify their perceptions of the videotaped material by telephoning at specified hours when training specialists are available for counseling.

It is of great importance, I believe, for the education profession to accelerate its concern for continuing professional growth. While college and university courses are useful, they are not the only—or perhaps even the best—method of ensuring the continuing development of the practitioner. The extension of professional competence can be pursued in a great many different ways; the effectiveness of these methods is likely to vary according to the particular circumstances and conditions that prevail. Much could be gained by a concerted effort to learn more about the best processes for the selection of particular continuing education activities.

DEVELOPING AUTONOMY

Autonomy in teaching can be traced back to the selection of the career. Teaching is one of the helping professions, and as such it offers distinct kinds of challenges and opportunities for self-satisfaction. The individual who enters teaching without exploring other vocational alternatives and without giving careful thought to the consequences of a professional life in the classroom has already abdicated a portion of his autonomy—he has not, in reality, exercised mature choice. This is not to say, of course, that college freshmen should always have determined their professional destiny. But, unhappily, there are many instances in which students delay the selection of a college major until the last moment—then register as prospective teachers of, say, English, merely because they have already accumulated most of the credentialing and licensing requirements. One must, I believe, have a deep-seated commitment to one's work in order to achieve the fullest measure of autonomy. It is when we believe strongly in the worth of what we are doing that we are most likely to take its challenges and opportunities with great seriousness, and most motivated to exercise a great degree of personal independence and imagination in becoming an autonomous professional.

True autonomy is heavily dependent upon the availability of a variety of learning opportunities— opportunities that vary both in their educational objectives and in their learning means. Autonomy extends, in other words, to the personal exercise of choice in determining which skills, and which understandings, are to be acquired. For example, some teachers, convinced that the Engelmann reading materials for young children are useful, may wish to acquire the techniques of operant conditioning essential to the program. Other teachers, in contrast, may believe that an inquiry approach to learning is more appropriate to their particular students and subject matter. Accordingly, their preference will be for technical skills involved in the effective guidance and management of classroom discussions. Still other teachers, interested in expanding learning opportunities beyond the walls of the classroom, may seek to become more familiar with activities that integrate learning in the school and community. For autonomy to flower, such alternatives must be available to the teaching profession. Unfortunately, our resources in this regard are still somewhat primitive. There is, consequently, yet further reason to believe that teacher continuing education must have a more potent program of research and development than heretofore has been the case.

In each of these choices one has a further opportunity for choice about the means, that is, the kind of educational activities he can carry on to attain these objectives. The illustrations presented earlier are only a few of the many possible means for learning that are or can be made available to teachers. Clearly, the school should seek to provide at least two or more ways that a teacher may learn each of these different kinds of behavior so that he may choose one that seems to him appropriate for his style of learning and the particular circumstances of his position. Feedback should be built into every program to aid the teacher to make further choices, to indicate unwise decisions made earlier, and to guide his efforts for continuing improvement. This feedback to the individual teacher should tell him how well he is doing, where he is having difficulty, and suggest a choice of ways by which to correct errors, overcome the difficulties, and make improvements.

The main emphasis of this chapter has been upon the need for systematic planning and development of programs of continuing education for teachers. Effective and efficient programs should focus on the needs of the school and also upon the development of autonomous teachers. With the rapidly changing society, the schools are facing new problems that require teachers with new attitudes, new understanding, and new skills. The job of in-service education is too big to be left to chance opportunities, and the enthusiasm, initiative, intelligence, and energy of teachers are too important to permit autonomy to be smothered by a mechanistic bureaucracy. It is possible for teachers to become involved in the analysis of the school's problems, in the identification of new competencies that must be acquired to carry out remedial strategies, and to select or devise a variety of ways to develop these competencies. Continuing education developed in this way is an aid to autonomous teachers, not a training scheme for slaves to the system.

editor's comments

THE TIMES have changed, Tyler tells us. New social needs have developed—and, consequently, schooling must address itself to different kinds of tasks. He, like other social scientists, forewarns that the educational rationale of the past is archaic; we need a new spirit and a new guiding philosophy—reflected in new policies and practices. He is especially concerned that the reach of education be broadened: "We must learn to reach children who have not been reached before, and to educate, beyond high school, youth from homes where no one has been to college before." Altogether, these are formidable challenges

—ones that likely cannot be accomplished mechanically through our present system. Imaginative change is mandatory.

Tyler sees in the immediate future a definitive test of the viability of a truly democratic, pluralistic society. Such a society will almost certainly demand a school system that is distinguished by diversity and multiformity. Three critical ambitions for the future are thus implicit: the public at large must be made aware of the need for such diversity; instructional materials and methods, tailored to different kinds of learners, must be designed; and the operational mechanics, for sustaining an educational system that can provide different "brands" of education according to individual students' needs, must be thought through.

Notably, the chapter takes an eclectic view of the teacher professional growth we most need for this kind of educational system. Tyler prescribes teachers who are knowledgeable about the homes and communities in which their students reside, who have learned effective ways in which to collaborate with parents and other community personages in the education of the young, who have acquired expertise in a variety of pedagogical skills, and, above all, who have learned—and can teach their students —the freedom and responsibility of *autonomy*. Autonomy, as Tyler describes it, means that "an individual has a good deal of control over his life; he has a wide range of choices; he knows enough about the probable consequences of each major possible course of action that he can make an informed choice." Crucial to the exercise of autonomy is the idea that knowledge of the "probable consequences" is the only rational basis for exercising informed choice. Genuine autonomy, moreover, is dependent upon an ability to see the larger picture, to go beyond the immediate situation. This sort of awareness, according to Tyler, is best achieved by both teacher and student through participation in problem-solving tasks. He seeks, in short, human beings who successfully control their own destiny.

To be autonomous, one must have acquired the ability to learn from alternative lessons. One must, from childhood on, have had repetitive practice in decision making, and in evaluating the consequences of decision choices. Tyler is convinced that children must learn this way of learning, with continuing guidance and support, with the teacher serving as a live model for students to emulate. He believes that children can successfully guide their own education—once they understand the school's expectations and the techniques to meet them—and set their own sequential learning tasks. The continuing education of teachers for this sort of educational model is of highest priority in the period ahead. As new learning environments are created, new instructional materials designed, and new programs initiated, all will come to naught if the teacher is not schooled in their intelligent use.

The author's conception of how best to approach continuing teacher education is both humanistic and pragmatic; he argues, for example, that in the case where 75 percent of the student population is making reasonable progress in learning, the need for such continuing education of teachers is relatively slight. It is in the cases where serious problems are being encountered—whether because of limited ability, atypical background, or emotional impediments—that the heaviest concentration of teacher retraining should occur. Tyler is suggesting that we direct our attentions, first, to the large, egregious problems upon which hinge the overall effectiveness of our educational programs; second, to the special continuing education and experiential needs of new teachers; and, third, to the necessity of allowing all teachers endless opportunity to develop their repertory of generalized technical skills.

Reduced to its essence, then, the corrective strategy he prescribes includes an identification of the problems, a consideration of alternate solutions, the creation of a learning system based upon the most promising options, and the subsequent training of teachers so that the new system can be used with intelligence and sensitivity.

In sum, Tyler's chapter paints a demanding, but optimistic, picture of the future. The continuing work of realigning the public school system with changing social realities must be pressed onward. In our time, this means that schools must overcome their predilection for giving only limited services to disadvantaged minorities, and begin to serve all youth. In seeking to accomplish these things, Tyler says, the surest path to success lies in the education and reeducation of teachers, the committed practitioners upon whom successful educational change depends.

3.

Howsoever one conceives of the schools, they serve, in one way or another, as preparation for adult life. For the present school generation, continued social crisis is inevitable. It is thus fitting that the problems of coping with crisis be a central element in the curriculum.

chapter 3
CONFRONTING A SOCIETY IN CONFRONTATION
Edward J. Meade, Jr.

I WISH IN THIS CHAPTER to set forth a proposal regarding the future role of teachers in our schools. For a philanthrapoid to offer, rather than review, a proposal is perhaps a strange reversal of protocol. Out of continuously reviewing the propositions of others, however, one invariably develops insights and a point of view of his own. The proposal is based on a deepseated conviction that changes in teaching are both necessary and inevitable.

For as long as we have had an American society, social critics, both foreign and domestic, have noted the flawed ways in which Americans seem to respond to social crisis. Our tendency, the critics say, is to oversimplify matters, reducing complex situations to shallow formulas, and to polarize on issues. Above all, we are taken to task for our failure to perceive the fine gradations between opposites; the American penchant is for ultimate solutions: either/or, yes/no, right/wrong, black/white. A preference for extremes, of course, is not uniquely an American cultural trait.

It is sufficiently characteristic, nonetheless, that we would do well to keep it in mind when we seek to resolve our dilemmas. For throughout our history there have been repeated instances in which we have been forced to moderate earlier excesses in action. And even where we stayed with our decision, the cost of too-narrow vision has always been high, if only because it precludes a consideration of alternatives.

Examples come readily to mind: during World War II, when the battle was beginning to tip in our favor, many Americans, our administration among them, concluded that the enemy was totally wrong and we were absolutely right; therefore, nothing less than "unconditional surrender" would do. In the early debates on the Vietnam War, the controversy revolved around two primary options: should we "go all out" or should we "pull out." Public opinion divided chiefly between those who contended that we should go all out and win, and those who favored complete and immediate withdrawal. Such one-sidedness, admittedly, occasionally leads to striking achievements. A decade or so ago our government committed itself to placing a man on the moon, preferably before the Russians could do so, and at whatever the necessary cost. We pursued the goal with awesome intensity and tenacity. Ultimately we did send a man to the moon, whatever the cost, and we did so well ahead of the Russians. We can turn for examples elsewhere in our history, to the books that have been banned from public library shelves, to the war internment of our Japanese citizens, to the loyalty oaths we demanded of university professors, to the era of McCarthyism, and to a great number of other instances in which we deprived ourselves of rational choice.

Whether or not this tendency toward ultimates

represents a typical American trait is not germane to the arguments I wish to advance. For the present purpose it suffices to say that overreaction and extremism have occurred in American life with some regularity. Hence, as we consider solutions to the problems of schooling, we ought rightly to be mindful of past sins. Unchanging commitment to an idea is not only irrational, but it also breeds intellectual poverty because it deprives the mind of free choice among possibilities.

Almost from its inception, our society has been involved periodically in one sort of confrontation or another. Traditionally, attitudes and beliefs have polarized as much as they seem to be doing today. There is, however, something significantly different about our current disputes: an infinitely larger portion of the body politic is actively involved in the issues. We appear to have become less content with representative government and more interested in an authentic participatory democracy. Thus, people of diverse class, race, and political conviction seem to take public issues personally. This, perhaps, is one of the more beneficent aspects of our technological accomplishments in mass communication. But what is most notable is that increased interest in public issues has divided rather than consolidated the nation. Now, the powerful drive of self-interest is far more likely to obscure a concern for the public good. Our military posture in the Middle East, for example, has one meaning for an investor in a defense industry, and quite another for a lad of draft age. It is this heightened self-interest that accounts in part for the dramatic upsurge of extremism.

It may well be that we have arrived at *the* age of confrontation. Not only are there the customary differences of opinion, but confrontation—as a social exercise—has itself become popular. Once the almost exclusive domain of the politician, deliberate controversy has now moved into the home, the church, the school, the street corner, business and industry, the courts, and, most dramatically, into the universities. For a large segment of the population, social serenity has become synonymous with decadence. It is not even necessary that the issues at stake be crucial; often they amount to no more than a negation of custom or a disaffirmation of accepted belief. Some of the confrontations, on the other hand, do have great significance. The counter-cultures, spawned by the changing times, have created a number of deep-seated conflicts. A brief reference to four such conflicts can be used to illustrate the dissonances that are characteristic of a society in social transition.

The first of these might be defined as a fundamental disharmony between "color" and "white." "Color" seems more appropriate than "black" because, increasingly, the once predominate confrontation between black and white has given way to a social war between the man of color and the man, if you will, of no color—the white. The confrontation sometimes resembles a contest between whites and non-whites, and often centers, not on a reasonable accommodation of differences, on compromise, or on the resolution of specific grievances, but rather on a more basic question as to who will dominate whom—who is to control whose destiny?

Another kind of confrontation also segregates the society, pitting people against one another and replacing old alliances with new rivalries. The aversion between father and son—what has been called the generation gap—is taking its own peculiar toll. In a sense, the dissension between the young and the old is less a matter of age than of life-style. Roughly half the nation's population is over twenty-five and the other half is under twenty-five. But the two social classes that are evolving are defined, not by physical age, but by point of view. Whether one is fifteen or fifty, one can identify with the "now" generation, ordering his life accordingly, or one can join with the old guard and value social conservatism.

A third example of confrontation in contemporary America might be labeled noninstitutional versus institutional. Overstating it, the clash is the historical opposition between revolutionary and reactionary outlook. There are those who maintain that our institutions and civil processes no longer serve the public cause and must therefore be destroyed. Their antagonists, conversely, believe that these institutions are the only safeguard against utter chaos, and, consequently, they must be perpetuated and used to reinforce the status quo. The latter reason that our traditional institutions have withstood the test of time, preventing catastrophe, and they thus offer an orderly and reasonable recourse to change if people will but have faith and conform to the American ethic. The radical view instead is that the traditional institutions have become instruments of social domination, not liberation, and that there is little hope for the society until they are demolished.

One more form of confrontation can be cited to demonstrate the broad spectrum of social unrest. There is a rapidly developing contradiction between what has been termed the *quality* of life as opposed to the *quantity* of life. The nation has flourished as a consequence of its remarkable capacity for productivity. We look with satisfaction to our ever-increasing gross national product, to the burgeoning stockpile of goods and services, to the impressive affluence of some of our citizens, and to the fact that we enjoy a higher living standard than virtually any other nation on earth. A disquieting note of increasing intensity, however, is beginning to be heard: there is a growing suspicion that the productivity, the affluence, and the material artifacts have, in point of fact, eroded the *quality* of life. The indictments span a broad front: industrial wastes pollute our environment; inflation bankrupts our economy; high salaries disrupt some of our public and private services, and, in general, greed overwhelms our sense of proportion. The issue, put plainly, is whether to accept a more livable life without some of the comforts we have learned to expect, or whether to further exploit our productive resources in order to provide more and more material benefits to more and more people.

These extremes, obviously, present tough opposites. While they may, to an extent, be overstated, they do illuminate the great necessity for rational choice in the period ahead. The reader will have little difficulty in finding other examples of social confrontation, of greater or lesser degree, which touch his own concerns. But what of the controversies within our own profession? What will result from our failure to solve past riddles as we attempt to deal with the new ones that now are emerging? The great debates regarding homogeneous and heterogeneous groupings are still with us. So, too, are the issues of arbitrary grading standards, departmentalized or self-contained classrooms, behavioral or nonbehavioral objectives, inductive or deductive learning, structured or nonstructured instruction, and the pros and cons of heuristic learning. Beyond these, there are the fresh dilemmas. Who shall control education, the citizen or the professional? Who shall teach, the trained instructor or the semitechnical aide? Is it better to teach children individually or in groups? And, to footnote the major issue in this volume, to what extent shall the school concern itself with the intellect and to what extent with the emotions?

This recital of the polarities that have formed within the society and within education set the stage for the proposal that follows. If dichotomies and extremist views are the hallmark of our time, what can and should the schools do with respect to preparing their clients to deal with confrontation? If controversy—in and out of the schools—is inevitable, what tack can educators take? To state the matter bluntly, if it is the business of the school to equip the child for life, and if, inevitably, life poses controversies and the need for decision making, what should teachers teach? How, in brief, do we best prepare students for the confrontations that lie ahead of them?

Presently, many schools subscribe to a doctrine of escapism. While the conflicts rage in the world outside, the classroom is a sheltered haven of intellectual tranquility. When issues are permitted to enter the classroom door, they tend to center around such matters as the length of hair and skirts. Occasionally, students are asked to consider political issues, discuss things a bit, and perhaps a mock "election" is held. Thus, our future citizens are educated.

All of the foregoing would seem to lead to three conclusions: first, in the time ahead, the effect of self-determinism will be increasingly important to the welfare of our society; second, the only alternative to confrontation is evasion; and third, the probability of achieving a value-free school is virtually nil.

To enlarge on the first of the three conclusions, the present state of affairs in the society gives genuine cause for concern. It is not just that we are in the midst of forced change; we appear to be desperately threatened by the need to even consider alternative life-styles. Most of us struggle to find ourselves the whole of our lives. In so doing, we fabricate a personal interpretation of the way things are. Often it does not matter whether the interpretation is valid or invalid, real or imagined; what matters, of course, is that it helps us cope with the dilemmas of our existence. Thus we fashion for ourselves a value pattern with which we can live. And once we learn to depend upon this pattern, it becomes sacrosanct. We stay with our ideas, in short, because there is a distinct payoff in doing so. Our beliefs are fed through self-interest. To do otherwise would be to submit to the painful anxiety of looking at ourselves afresh and to endure readjustment.

But times change. The young, unencumbered by a knowledge of the world that was, are constructing for themselves new and radically different interpretations of life. Worse, they are compelling us to face our social order head-on and to reexamine its worth. In return, we find their own virgin interpretations of "the good life" upsetting. We worry about their preoccupation with hedonism, about their tendency to find the "good, true, and beautiful" in needles, about their tolerance for violence, about their concern (however well-intentioned) for the environment and about their preference for words rather than deeds.

Nonetheless, they have successfully penetrated our veneer. It is now more difficult to be self-satisfied and more easy to be self-suspicious. The young have driven us to self-confrontation. This, perhaps, accounts for our sudden interest in sensitivity groups and similar activities through which we can reconsider the meaning of life. More than ever before, we are preoccupied with self-knowledge. It is as if we have suddenly realized that man is weakened by unused potential and we must, therefore, take stock of our resources.

As a result, the quest for self-knowledge is likely to become an important aspect of schooling, and properly so. Both teacher and learner will need to give greater credence to the fact that the quality of life is heavily dependent upon the choices we make. Of even greater importance, they will need to recognize that retreating from issues and circumventing decisions is false security. For all of us, anxiety and inward crisis are an expensive price to pay. In the long run, however, they probably are a good value. For without self-appraisal we are reduced to secondhand values.

The alternative to confrontation, to touch upon the second conclusion, is avoidance. During the past decade the ebb and flow of the social scene has made it clear that evasion provides only temporary relief; the problems do not go away. We have yet, for example, to solve the problem of equal educational opportunity; we still have not found a way to meet the pluralistic educational expectations of different segments of the society; and financing the cost of public schooling is becoming increasingly difficult. We shift from one crisis to another, gaining momentary respite, but they return again and again to haunt us.

Escapism is one of our common weaknesses. Our predilection for newness stems, in part, from a pervasive belief that it is better to invent something new than to repair something old. The great investment in planned innovation has not produced a uniformly high return, however, and it would appear that our backs are now to the wall and we must therefore confront rather than evade.

The necessity for making a satisfactory transition from the culture of the past to the culture of the future is hard upon us. We cannot survive the generation gap forever, and if the society is to flourish there must be a fundamental realignment, which can only come about through a direct confrontation with the crucial issues. The problem, obviously, is that because we see the issues differently we also see different solutions. The dimensions of the difficulties we face with respect to social education is therefore evident. The society will become increasingly pluralistic. It will be divided, moreover, not only by ethnic and class differences but by philosophical ones as well. As a result, the dichotomy between individualism and the collective good, between "doing your own thing" and "doing the society's thing" will enlarge. And, as a consequence, there will be more issues, more conflicts, and a correspondingly greater need to negotiate rationally among alternatives.

The implications for the school are clear. The curriculum must be opened to controversial issues. Teachers must challenge and be challenged. Not only must they scrutinize their own beliefs, bred out of their experiences, but they must also ask their students to do the same. It is well to remember that what we take to be "right" is largely dependent upon our experience. Every experience, furthermore, is personal. Thus, it seems to me, there is a common ground between the negotiation and decision making essential to the resolution of personal problems and social issues. This common ground is the fulcrum between personal authenticity and civic responsibility.

The third conclusion, that having to do with the impossibility of a value-free school, follows logically. It would be foolish to assume that, through schooling, we can rid people of their private value schemes and equip them to respond to their life situations impersonally. They cannot, in short, be taken from their individualism, and they cannot be made to embrace ready-made values. Through rational consideration of different possibilities and disparate needs and views, however, they can be taught to suspect any self-held idea that seems absolutely essential to their happiness. As Jones and Rubin repeatedly note elsewhere in this volume, teachers and students alike must recognize that human decisions are not based on reason alone—feeling and emotion too have their effect.

We ought, in sum, to be able to make the school a place in which problems are illuminated instead of camouflaged, in which self-understanding and social understanding are parts of a whole, and in which confrontation and the analysis of conflicts are orderly and sanative processes. But such a state of affairs, many contend, can never be.

There are various rationales in the standard educational literature as to why this remove from the real world is essential for schools. A common argument, for example, is that because the schools are society's acculturing agency, they must abstain from exposing students to our social ills. Another notion in wide currency is that schools must remain "detached" so that students can gain an "objective" picture of the social scene. Some theorists have also argued that public education ought to deal in fundamental skills and information. Without a background of basic knowledge, the student is incapable of thinking intelligently about an issue; schooling, therefore, ought not to exaggerate its proper role. My own reasoning leads to a rather different conclusion.

Is not society's purpose in maintaining educational institutions that of improving human welfare? The investment in an educated citizenry is justified chiefly by the conviction that men ought to enable their pro-

geny to improve the culture, perpetuating desirable
elements and modifying or eliminating undesirable
ones. By developing individual capacity, schools seek
to better the lot of mankind. Or, as Kenneth Boulding has said, "What formal education has to do is to
produce people who are fit to be inhabitants of the
planet."[1] How can we possibly produce "fit inhabitants" if we avoid a rigorous examination of the way
things are?

Many persons, in and out of education, have com-
mented on the lack of reality in American schools,
especially our secondary schools. Looking at our
schools, who would ever believe that they came from
a history of adventurous exploration and of the confrontation and testing of knowledge against the realities of the world? All of these qualities are a part of
what is the American heritage and yet the American
school seems not endowed with them.

We seem to close out reality in much of what we
do in schools. We teach knowledge and require that
it be learned without asking ourselves or the students
to apply it to themselves and their realities. We even
discourage the confrontation of knowledge versus
knowledge. We assume that the school is not the
place for decisions to be made. In fact, our behavior
assumes that decisions, if made, are made *for* the
students. Decisions, we reason, are made by people
who already have been through school and who are
"educated." Is one simply in school only to "learn"
and not also to "live?"

One of our great errors has been to assume that
young children do not need to make significant decisions until later in their lives. The events of the past

1.   Kenneth Boulding, "Ecology & Environment," *Trans Action*
(New Brunswick, N.J.: Rutgers State Univ., March, 1970) p. 44.

two decades have made it abundantly clear that the young *do* make important choices, early on, and that very often these choices have a profound impact on the remainder of their lives. A lad who flunks junior high school becomes a high school dropout, and in time matriculates to drug addiction. The most consequential of the decisions made by the young, of course, rarely have to do with schooling; they relate, for the most part, to more serious things—to the matters that govern one's sense of adequacy and fulfillment. When these needs become more elusive, as they seem to have done in the recent past, the decisions of young people tend more and more to extremes. It is almost as if the mid-course, the halfway point, is no longer a viable alternative.

As most professional decision makers know, good decisions generally do not go to extremes; more often than not, the greatest benefit lies in compromising between opposites. Such compromise, however, comes from reasoning through alternatives. Good decisions, in other words, are reached through a process of mediation—self-negotiation—wherein one identifies the various alternatives available, predicts the probable consequences of each, and reaches his decision. Thus, healthy choice is built out of valid evidence filtered through one's value scheme. If, then, the young make decisions, and if the quality of these decisions is often left to chance rather than to design, the schools are indeed selling their students short.

Boulding again is instructive on the point, although he refers to conflict, whereas I prefer the more positive term confrontation. He writes:

> It is well-managed conflicts, not the absence of conflicts that make for success in marriage, in industrial relations, and in party politics, and

underlie almost all creativity in both art and
science. This is something that formal education
does not seem to teach very well.[2]

Why must it be so, we might ask?

Can we not arrange formal education so that it
prepares students to manage controversy, conflict,
and confrontation? Can we not devise a curriculum
that gives each student a personalized system of decision making, one providing cumulative practice in
the orderly resolution of issues? Surely the capacity
to deal intelligently with reality and to overcome
problems is at least as important as much of the subject matter we now teach. To do these things, however, it will be necessary to allow controversy to intrude
upon the presently suppressed curricula.

There are those who take alarm at the notion that
conflict, even intellectual conflict, ought to be encouraged in the schools. Such fears are largely
groundless. Our political scientists, psychologists,
and sociologists all tell us that some conflict is in fact
necessary to stable relationships; the institution that
stifles internal conflict becomes weaker, not stronger.
Conflict, at manageable levels, and in tolerable
forms, serves to solidify relationships and to clarify
options. It is for this reason that our democracy
elects to provide both the far left and the far right
with public platforms; the extreme positions increase
the range of choice in between.

This endorsement of the social utility of conflict
does not imply, obviously, that conflict is good;
rather, it implies that in organized group life a certain amount of conflict is both natural and desirable.
The chief application of this principle to the schools

2. Kenneth Boulding, *op. cit.*, p. 43.

is not that it offers a way to make students more cohesive, because cohesiveness alone is not our educational purpose. Let a winning football team fulfill that institutional requirement. Nor is the principle useful in guaranteeing that schools that tolerate, or even promote, controlled conflict will siphon off some student aggressiveness, thereby making youth more manageable at home, more placid in the streets, and more amenable at the draft boards. The importance of this finding from social psychology is that it tells us that because healthy, normal group experiences include confrontation, the suggestion that teachers utilize confrontation in their classroom lessons is neither dangerous nor irresponsible. Indeed, what is far more shocking is the idea that confrontation should not be allowed to enter the schoolroom.

By way of summation, it would be appropriate to set forth the proposal I alluded to at the outset. Essentially, it is a proposal of five parts:

First, I propose that the curriculum emphasize the rational consideration of controversial issues. Issues —questions for which good answers are not readily apparent—can be made a common thread in the fabric of instruction. Whether the learning task is that of testing for an unknown substance in the chemistry laboratory, ferreting out the factors that contribute to economc depression, comparing the stylistic differences between two pieces of literature, or determining the best strategy to use in a basketball game, the basic processes for analyzing and resolving issues can be taught and learned, and students can cumulatively improve their reasoning skills.

Second, I propose that the curriculum equip the child, year by year, to become a more adept decision maker. The need to choose, and the fear of choosing unwisely, together account for more anxiety than most of life's other requirements. To be sure, we cannot guarantee that correct decisions always will be made, but we can increase the likelihood and we can reduce the concomitant tensions. There are many ways to accomplish specified ends and each has its own ramifications. Wherever these ramifications can be anticipated and thought through, decision-making ability can be enhanced. To write an essay, the student must decide upon a point of view. To select a novel for reading, he must decide upon his dominant interests. To plan a budget, he must decide upon his priorities. To design a physics project, he must decide upon his resources. Throughout the whole of the instructional arena, in short, there are rich opportunities for teaching decision making. What is required is that these opportunities be exploited, and that decision making itself be treated as a primary educational target rather than as a by-product of other objectives.

Third, I propose that the curriculum provide decision-making training for those situations in which a limited amount of evidence is available. When there is a great deal of data with which to predict probable outcomes, decision making is comparatively easy. It is when necessary data is absent that estimating consequences is hazardous. Robert Finch once described the problem this way:

> One must master what is perhaps the most difficult of tasks: to make decisions at times before all the facts are in. A political official has to act, and often he must act to protect lives and property, before he is quite sure of the terrain. In such circumstances, if he were to wait until all the facts are known—*until the future is part of*

the past—he would lose his capacity to influence the course of events.[3]

It is not just the politician who finds it necessary to make decisions when elements in the formula are missing. It happens so with parent and child, husband and wife. It ought to be possible for the school to provide its pupils with a backlog of decision-making experience. Out of such experience comes the sharpened intuition that improves the quality of our "educated guesses." Admittedly, schools and teachers must impart knowledge. But technical knowledge has its limitations, for few decisions are based solely on hard facts. Indeed, the school may be one of the few places where an individual can, in safety, practice the processes of decision making. It is in the school, therefore, that the individual must learn to recognize and manage the emotional and intellectual aspects of free choice.

Fourth, I propose that the curriculum deal with the major confrontations ongoing in the society. The schools cannot serve the public interest by retreating from the crucial problems of the time. If our goal is an educated citizenry, a case might even be made for asking that the schools confront society itself. Only when the school is willing to allow its students to examine the issues being contested outside its wall, to analyze the conflicts dividing the society, dividing people, and, for that matter, dividing the individual, will we achieve an informed and competent body politic. We need a curriculum, in brief, that makes it possible to have what Henry Steele Commager once called "free enterprise in ideas."

3. Robert Finch, *The School and The Democratic Environment* (New York: Columbia University Press, 1970), p. 28.

Finally, I propose that the curriculum make it possible for all learners to acquire the delicate art of self-negotiation. The stream of life, after all, is an unending process of negotiating with one's self. Man is too often a self-defeating animal. The current style of life in America—the hate and violence, the divorces, the suicides, the alienation—are hardly a tribute to the educational system. Knowledge, of the kind dispensed by the school, does not always beget wisdom. We may be somewhat successful at teaching students to pass our classroom tests but we do less well at teaching them to pass life's tests. School ought to be a place where a person gets to know himself. It ought to be a place where one learns to confront personal issues and to resolve them as well as possible. In large measure, our difficulties in negotiating with others stem from the earlier failure to come to terms with ourselves. Knowledge of self and knowledge of others are of a piece. Both are essential to individual health and societal health. They may well be the school's most important business.

editor's comments

MEADE BEGINS his analysis with the assumption that societal crisis is inevitable in a rapidly changing society. His concern is therefore not with the elimination of social stress, but rather with the development of healthy ways of accommodating to it. Like Tyler, his approach is pragmatic, reflecting a belief that it is not crisis but the way in which men respond to it that makes the difference.

One senses that Meade is almost relieved that we finally "have arrived at *the* age of confrontation." Now, at long last, the way is perhaps clear to deal rationally with issues and conflicts. The inability to recognize the fine lines between opposites, the preference for ultimate solutions, and the extremism and overreaction that Meade describes have been mirrored in the microcosm of the schoolroom. And in seeking to achieve objectivity and to avoid a bias in favor of one posture or another, we have adopted policies designed to circumvent a consideration of the critical issues on which public opinion is divided. In a series of telling arguments, Meade recommends first, that we acknowledge the ubiquitous nature of controversy, and, second, that we bring it, foursquare, to the classroom. Because, as the author notes, "the probability of achieving a value-free school is virtually nil," why fight a foredoomed battle? Instead, why not accept the fact that adults must deal rationally with difficult value decisions and begin, as early on as possible, to prepare children for the conflicts that lie ahead.

In these regards, Meade's hopes for a better school system rest chiefly on the achievement of three goals: increasing the individual's capacity for self-determinism; using rather than avoiding confrontation; and allowing for a free play of values within the curriculum. To reach these will require both instructional experiences to prepare students to manage confrontation, conflict, and controversy, and experiences that provide schooling in decision making. Moreover, such education must include, as well, practice in making decisions where the supporting evidence is limited.

These are, he acknowledges, profoundly difficult tasks. For most of us, the immediate temptation is to select controversial issues that are sufficiently removed from reality so as to not produce discomforting anxiety—thus insuring that the experience will be virtually meaningless. There is an alternative and equally great temptation to avoid reality entirely and to substitute games and simulations. It is precisely these temptations that the writer most wants us to avoid; indeed, he is sublimely clear on the matter: "We ought, in sum, to be able to make the school a place in which problems are illuminated instead of camouflaged, in which self-understanding and social understanding are parts of a whole, and in which confrontation and the analysis of conflict are orderly and sanative processes." In short, Meade refuses to believe, as many others have, that such a school is an impossibility.

He is convinced that most rational adults wish to prepare their children to deal with difficult decisions; and, moreover, that it is hopelessly naive to assume that because we do not treat our social ills in the curriculum, our students will remain unaware. To the contrary, the young may have a shrewder understanding of our social dilemmas than their elders. Finally, the chapter makes it clear that to assume that young people are not already faced with the need to resolve difficult decisions is equally specious; the proverbial dilemma of wishing to have one's cake and to eat it as well serves as a case in point. If we proceed logically and sanely, taking pains to make the adult community aware of what we are trying to accomplish—and why—Meade thinks we will encounter far less resistance to the goals than we imagine.

It is hard to contradict Meade's persuasive rhetoric because, to my knowledge, the procedures he suggests have never—at least, in the way he suggests—been tried and found wanting. Indeed, I believe that knowledgeable experts on the classroom would be inclined to agree that, in the hands of a sensitive teacher, everything he urges is eminently possible. Nonetheless, to pursue the course recommended much must be done in the way of preparation. We must convince public and practitioner that an honest curriculum has its advantages. We must develop instructional materials that treat conflict and controversy in realistic and unbiased fashion. We must create in-school situations that awaken children to values and decisions that affect the quality of their lives, and immerse them in controlled decision-making situations that generate some anxiety and inward crisis. And we must help them to perceive that these unavoidable stresses and tensions are best resolved, not by escapism, but by a direct confrontation and a rational resolution.

In the previous chapter, Tyler wrote of the need for

continuing teaching education. What Meade envisions—
equipping teachers to manage intellectual and emotional
conflicts in an orderly classroom—is, at minimum, a massive undertaking for any training venture. But, like many
of the other radical proposals that appear in the book, it is
well within the range of feasibility. If we believe that a
change is both possible and worthwhile, there is a moral
obligation to try—the difficult, after all, is not the impossible.

4.

The history of man's progress is etched in a cumulative sequence of social revolutions. In a sense, each generation must fashion a society to fit its time. The school, therefore, must equip its clients to separate the important from the trivial, and to find those values that are of greatest consequence.

chapter 4
REVOLUTION
WITHIN REASON
·
Michael Scriven

IN THE TWENTY-FIRST CENTURY, we can be sure about one aspect of curriculum debate: It will still involve many of the same dilemmas we are discussing here. There will probably be some tiresome historians around arguing that everything that looks new at that time is really just what they did at Columbia University's Teachers College in the 1920s, or Philadelphia's celebrated Parkway School in the 1960s. Nevertheless, there will be new things in education because small differences in approaches often have big differences in effects, and because things in education cannot be assessed independently of their social context, and *that* will surely be different. The "critical thinking" of the thirties isn't the same as the training in value analysis of the sixties, either in detail or in significance—and the worth of new approaches depends on the details and on their relationship to the other alternatives available in the curriculum and in the society at large.

The historian's "put down" of innovation must be viewed with caution. But even more caution must be reserved for the faddists, the arbiters of fashion, the antihistorical approach. We all find something attractive in the novel, even in the end just because it is novel; and we all find it a little uncomfortable to be wearing what is no longer fashionable, or to be unable to discuss the latest "-ism." So we are far too likely, in education, to jump too soon to the new, to discard too readily the old. If the twenty-first century is to be survived, or even attained, it will only be because we have overcome much of our present tendency to act as if curriculum or methods were like hairstyles. But I am not arguing for crusty conservatism of the usual variety. For that makes a value of the old—no less a disaster than its opposite. It, too, is highly uncritical—in this instance, uncritical about the past. Maturity can lead to divorce as well as reconciliation; to revolution as well as restraint.

MATURITY

Maturity in this society and in the curriculum, which is—perhaps better than most of us realized— its microcosm, will require a remarkable development of our critical abilities and our willingness to act on them. That development must occur in us, the teachers, as well as in our students. I do not say it must first occur in us. We now know very well that our students have taught many of us more about teaching than we learned in the course of what is amusingly referred to as our professional training as teachers. But this increase in maturity should occur in us, and it should be the key goal in the schools of education as well as in the classroom. How do you teach maturity? Perhaps we can best approach that question by first stressing some contrasts, by talking around the subject for a while, because it isn't an accident that we educators cannot rattle off a generally accepted definition of maturity, let alone a curriculum for teaching it. We cannot do any better with concepts such as *truth* or *virtue* or *scientific method,* and it is not because they are empty notions. It is simply that they are framework notions. Demands to define them are harder to handle than particular requests involving the same notions, in the same way that a request to justify a map's projection is harder to handle than requests to point out a particular place on the map. We do not have too much difficulty in recognizing maturity in a student—in written work and in conversation—though there is substantial disagreement and some of this is ineluctable. The situation is similar to that with respect to the term *intelligence.* The concept is workable—up to a point and for some tasks—but controversial, because it is important and not to be dismissed as vague and confused.

THE HERO APPROACH

Let us back off for a moment and look at some other conceptions of the curriculum that have had substantial support, and let us relate them to the theme of maturity. The two points made so far that bear on maturity concern sensitivity to the valuable— as opposed to the novel or to the established—and courage to stand by the judgment. Both of these involve affective considerations as well as cognitive ones. But whatever their individual components, both judgement and courage are necessary. It is clear that we have made little effort to teach the second and have been much surprised to discover that independence does not grow naturally in the environment of our society, especially as reflected in our schools. We supposed, I think, that reading about the courage of great men in history would inspire our students to emulate them. At best it inspires them to wish they could emulate them. But we never even capitalized on that motivation, we let it die in dreams.

And this was perhaps not entirely contrary to our unconscious wishes, because we may have dimly perceived that the heroes of past ages, translated into contemporary idiom, would be the worst kind of troublemakers. The classic example of this is the intelligent analysis of Christ as a hippie of his time, which was so shocking to the U.S. Army that it dismissed the editor of *Stars and Stripes* for reprinting it. The only good heroes are dead heroes.

Now one reason for that view is that it is so much easier to identify heroes long after they are dead. In the flesh they tend to smell a little sweaty and sound a little revolutionary. But sanctified by history, they are also sanitized by distance; quite safe, specimens and not subversives. Notice that the hero approach destroys both cognitive and affective learning opportunities. There is no need for discrimination—history has done that for you. And there is no need for action. The poor fellow no longer needs followers. He or she is dead. Sterilized, beatified, and useless—educationally speaking. The resurrection of the dead by "reliving" history as it was—the bitter struggles of imperfect wretches like ourselves and our contemporaries—is not just a task for the devotee of truth, the research historian. It is the only task that can convert pap into education.

I shall turn first to the concept of the curriculum that is most closely connected with the Hero Approach. The methods-oriented version of this suggests that the best way the child can become a good citizen is by exposure to a good example, namely the teacher. The back side of this coin is the vicious doctrine that teachers are to be released if they exhibit human divergences from the mean, ranging from short skirts to divorce, from political activism to smoking pot. Not only was the teacher supposed to be a hero, but he was not supposed to be human. It is not entirely surprising that the results of such pressures should have been the reduction of the ideal teacher to a social nonentity.

The subject matter consequence of the Hero Approach was rationalized in terms of "transmission of our cultural values." And this is of particular interest because it has appeared recently that such an approach, which is open to the gravest objections at first sight, does have a second line of defense. I do not find the usual version convincing. In my view, it is not the task of the curriculum to pass on the values or the mores of the culture. In the first place, it is far from clear that they are worth passing on, and in the second, we don't have any idea how to do it well. That is no reason not to try to find how to do it, but it is a reason against founding a curriculum on it now. And there is a third reason. It is entirely immoral to suppose we have any right to pass on values to other human beings, because passing on in this context means indoctrination. The only right we have, by the time the student gets to the schoolroom, is to teach him how to decide for himself on a values system.

THE RATIONAL APPROACH

This does not mean that we teach the child the rational approach, and thereby indoctrinate. It means that we offer the approach, examine it, describe it, try it, and—at the same time—provide a similar service for other approaches. "In kindergarten, are we going to offer the rational method and other approaches for children to consider? What are they supposed to be at that level? Philosophers?"

No, we are not going to start the philosophical discussion at the kindergarten level, only specific examples of its application; that is, we can give the children a chance to try planning against nonplanning and reflection versus reaction—in different areas. And there are other things to do. It is useful for children of this age to have some of the basic skills and some social experience, and teaching children the three Rs and some media skills is not violating their freedom to choose—if it is done by a rational teacher interested in teaching rationality as well as reading. As the students become more interested in asking questions about the way we run things in the classroom, and the way things are run in the outside world, we become even more committed to showing and discussing alternative possibilities. Of course, with some students, and with some of these questions, this may mean the kindergarten; with others, it may not be until much later. There is no point at all in talking about what is to be done when in the curriculum, as if it must happen at the same time for all students. It is a presupposition of any kind of education for the future that in one way or another it should be individualized, and individualization may affect sequencing as well as starting point.

TEACHER ROLES

I am trying to convey a sense of the vendor role that I think we as teachers should have. We are entitled to offer certain kinds of goods, and we are entitled to put these in as good a light as their supporters would suggest, just as long as the opposition gets a hearing. Not equal time, because the opposition is not, as far as we can tell, worth equal time. But that view may be our own prejudice, and the only way to prevent its becoming a prejudice of the society against which a revolution must eventually be fought is to make sure that the next generation gets a look at the alternatives, early in the game before we have brainwashed them, and also later, when they become more sophisticated about the matters involved. We are salesmen, but there is no contradiction in the idea that we can also teach students to view salesmen with some reservations, including those salesmen that sell them a way to evaluate salesmen! It is hard, but it is not impossible, and it is crucial for the scientist to be an enthusiast for his own theories and to make certain that his students will originate better ones.

There has lately been a good deal of talk about the teacher changing his or her role to that of resource instead of authority. I am suggesting something more radical—the switch to antiauthority. The school has no need to be in the role of culture conveyor, partly for the reasons mentioned but also because of an additional and independently overwhelming one, namely, the culture already does a tremendous job of indoctrination outside the classroom. So I think that the school has an important task of teaching resistance to this indoctrination by the culture. This means teaching the skills of autonomous judgment; for this training is what is most lacking in the outside culture. Now the teacher is an authority, too, and it is hypocritical to act as if she or he lacks the role's admittedly limited social powers as well as certain superior knowledge. So the way to describe this new role is to say that the teacher is an antiauthority, not a nonauthority, meaning that he or she is a special kind of authority, a specialist in the training of students against exploitation by the Establishment's natural inertia, the power of success and the pressures of those seeking it. Because it is abundantly clear that the teacher has for long been one of the exploiting group in many cases—also, of course, one of the exploited—it must be clear that the new role requires that he or she has to be willing and able to make the new training self-applicable. This is indeed a hard task, but it is the only challenge that matters. Far from being instruments of socialization, as such, the teachers must become the defenses against the depersonalization that has too often been identified as the first step to socialization, in the school as well as in boot camp, implicitly in the actual treatment of "troublemakers" as well as explicitly in the armed services. We have talked ego support and acted as ego crusher too long. We have seen the school as supplementing social teaching but have not seen that this means some antisocial teaching.

SUBJECT MATTER

Just as there is a need for a radical change in the role of the teacher and of his or her self-concept, so there is a need for a radical change in the subject matter. The halfway house is the transformation of the usual subject matter into something worth the time and related to the new goal of antiindoctrination or antisocialization, or—in a stronger sense than before—self-development. In any circumstance where one cannot manage the full switch, one will have to settle for what is both possible and feasible. Some of the recent curricula—for example, the Harvard Project social studies materials—are an immense step beyond the usual materials and a brilliant practical solution to the curriculum constraints in most schools. But the real subject matter must of course be the society itself—not as a topic in the usual sense, but as the stinking, charming, changing thing that it is and seems to be to the student—and not only the society but also his relation to it, and his attitudes to it, and thus ultimately his attitudes toward himself and others. If that takes T-groups, among other things, then that is what we ought to be doing in the classroom in the twenty-first century. (I rather think we can move to something considerably more sophisticated by that time, but there will be something from the same arena.) If it takes field trips, then that is where we will be during school hours; but these field trips are likely to go on for some time—maybe a day or two, or a week or two, or a month or two, or a year. If it takes social action projects, that is what the social studies class will do, maybe during election campaigns, maybe during the harvest, maybe at war or in jail.

Behind all this there is still a single conception: the conception of the teacher as the defender of the student, as the builder of his defenses, as the provider of what the family and the society usually undermine—the basis for his independence.

IDEOLOGY

It is not hard to describe what I have been saying in a quite different vocabulary. For example, it can be described in the vocabulary of the right wing: it is an emphasis on basic education plus an absolute rejection of one kind of indoctrination that rightly worries the right wing; it is an emphasis on independence, on individuality, on the rights of the individual. It can also be described in the vocabulary of the progressive educator. It can be described in the vocabulary of the radical educator. About all this shows is that these vocabularies are remarkably flexible, and the approach very loosely defined so far. And it is equally clear that proponents of these views, at least some of them, will have no difficulty in finding features of my suggestions to complain about.

There can really be nothing new in the future of education if we talk about what happens in a sufficiently general way. In one sense, what is new is always the same: it is the students. What is old is always the same: it is the faculty. And the problem is always the same: it is to help the students become old and help the faculty renew. One way to do it is to get across the idea that each year is a new subject matter, one that must be studied by the staff and discussed with the students. That is no reason to think that the perspective of our history in this country cannot illuminate the new events, that the halfway house is not also necessary. It is no reason to think that the contents of the curriculum are no longer of any value. It is just that we have to forget the idea that school is to prepare students to discuss these things. They are already discussing some of these things whether we help or not—but worse, they are already being corrupted as far as future discussions of these things are concerned by the uncriticized and uncritical discussions that go on in their homes and with their friends, and they have to be "saved" from just one situation—being unable to discuss them in a way that can lead them to their own decisions about them. The Jesuit of legend says, "Give me the child until he is seven and I'll have him for the rest of his life." We get the child before he is seven, and our duty is to make it possible for him to have the rest of his life. So far we have done more to close his eyes than to open them, more to incorporate him than to arm him, and this turns out to be no better way to defend our freedom than his.

Now the approach supported here is close to anarchy in its political presuppositions, for it has none. If anything besides anarchy comes out of it, it comes because it stands on its own two feet, not because it is given a good plug or supported by an effective brainwashing program in the classroom. In a very clear sense, the political aim of this approach is to encourage each generation to find its own form of government, to be willing to clear the board and work out the rules of the game they want to play, making what concessions they must to the old and feeble because these will one day be them. It is not our place to pass on our rules, in a country committed to real freedom. We have been fighting our dead issues with their young lives too long to argue that our practices are the best lesson of experience. So I am giving arguments for revolutions yet unborn, but also for a stability yet unknown—if it is the way that seems best suited to the times that belong to our students. The pathetic idea that they will not be able to work out a way to run the country unless they are indoctrinated with the way we have been doing it, with all its wretchedness, is the ultimate form of insecurity about its worth. To make your children do what you did because that will make you feel that it was the right way to do it, is like winning an election by killing the other candidates, a false vote of confidence indeed. And yet I believe that has been part of the explanation of the backlash. It is odd that we should have been so willing to argue for "learn by doing" in every area except that of developing autonomous judgment; I do not consider it accidental. It is odd that we should have been so strong on the idea of the free marketplace of ideas in every area except the schools; it is too much to suppose this is a coincidence. I think that we have given up exactly those ideas that the founding fathers exhibited, and retained only their words. The preservation in our laws of some of the substance of their conclusions has in fact given many of us an illusory sense of continuity, a dangerous sense of safety, that may even now be on the point of betraying us completely. We can only be saved, not by automatic revolution, but by opening up the possibility of revolution, by rejecting the automatism of rejecting it. Even if revolution were not an obvious candidate for consideration as a solution to social ills, it is the last frontier. We have closed out the others and we should not be surprised to find the next generation going on to the only one that is left; or right; or central. To make violence the new pornography is to incite it and for that reason stupid—though not for that reason alone. Worse still, it guarantees support for the old pornographers, the theorists of yesterday's revolutions—for they are the only suppliers if their trade is made illicit.

The approach here is revolutionary in that it contemplates revolution, and violent revolution at that, as simply one of the options, no more and no less. It is also rational in that it argues for this conclusion, and argues for the use of reason in making the decision. But it is not rational in the stereotyped sense of putting reason on a pedestal. It is epistemologically just as revolutionary as it is politically. Reason itself must earn its place in each generation, or it will have no place at all, only the rhetoric of one. If reason begins to regard emotion with askance and we find that the effects are bad for people, then it is time to shed that form of "reason" and work out a new one. Reason is no more than the best way to the truth— and no less. It has no more specific description; the rest is the trappings of the times, just as the forms of government are no guarantee of justice and their absence no proof of evil.

EPISTEMOLOGY

Reason is the best route to truth. Yes, but whose truth? Are we not still stacking the cards? No—as long as we are using the language in its usual sense. We start any discussion by agreeing on some way of distinguishing true from false in some cases. For example, we might start by agreeing that it is raining outside because we can see it through the windows, and that it is not raining inside. Given only that kind of agreement, we not only can make the case for reason as the best route to truth, we must make it, in different ways to different students and in different courses, but make it a hundred times in any child's education. It is a pretty important point and if we cannot get it across, the student will renege on it when he needs it most. It is not religious dogma, though. Maybe it is just a handy approximation that works in most cases—maybe in nearly all, maybe in all. We will have to sort out the puzzles about artistic truth and drug visions and ESP and the black experience and intuitions for ourselves and with our students. Not because they are philosophically interesting, which they are, but because we have been so dogmatic about them—one way or the other—that we have stopped teaching and students have stopped learning about them. And now they have revolted against reason, in favor of art or Consciousness III or psychedelia—rightly so, and overdue at that. For they were taught dogma from which comes no understanding.

To repeat, reason is the best route to truth. Perhaps it is not even a good approximation; we shall have to see. But certainly the claim is an evaluative one. The real kicker is in the term *best*. There have to be standards of judgment, or merit, or there cannot be any way to tell the best. And those standards must be worked out; they cannot themselves be laid down, with just the voice of authority, for then we have only postponed the arguments to the day when someone feels like asking why we should accept *this* authority. Rationality leads to values; it does not assume them uncritically. The strength of the rational approach resides precisely in its ubiquity and its fecundity, not in its technology. And the time has come to learn all that again.

CRITICISMS

Recently, some of those who are or have been among the leading proponents of reason and the rational approach have come to spurn it, or at least their interpretation of it, either explicitly or implicitly. Among the most important and most representative of these are Donald Oliver and Mary Jo Bane, who wrote "Is Reasoning Enough?"[1] and Joseph Schwab, who wrote "The Practical: A Language for Curriculum."[2] In what follows, I shall take up some of the points writers in these camps make and see if I can convince the reader, and perhaps even them, that the suggestions they make can best be understood as recommendations for a refined or an enlarged sense

1. D.W. Oliver and M.J. Bane, "Moral Education: Is Reasoning Enough?" in G.M. Beck, B.S. Crittenden, and E.V. Sullivan (Eds.), *Moral Education: Interdisciplinary Approaches* (Toronto: University of Toronto Press, 1971).

2. Joseph J. Schwab, "The Practical: A Language for Curriculum," (Washington, D.C.: Center for the Study of Instruction, National Education Association, 1970).

of reason, not for something else; for a revolution within reason and not a revolution against it. The issue is, I believe, critical. The shape of education from here on will really depend on the extent to which its administration and its curriculum opt for a rational approach, rather than for power politics and awareness baths. The needed change will not happen unless our priorities are both clear and strong.

Oliver and Bane write:

> We assume that man is or can be a rational animal; that he seeks greater complexity or maturity in the manipulation of verbal arguments; that he can become engaged in more abstract social and political issues in a somewhat impartial or impersonal way without such a deep mistrust of his own psyche that it will warp his perceptions.[3]

But I believe the basic presuppositions are wrong. Let me lay my alternative interpretation on the table. I think these arguments, for which I have a very high regard, only assume that most men can become more rational, and that increased subtlety in the analysis of complex problems sometimes leads to a solution. I prefer a more modest assumption, one that carries less risk, because it has partially been established by empirical and logical proof: by saddling the rational approach with other, more questionable, claims, it becomes possible to reject rationality more easily. I think this does us no favor.

Many people of this persuasion also seem to believe that rationality creates motivational and gener-

3. Oliver and Bane, *op. cit.*, p. 260.

alization problems. They therefore suggest devices
that may defeat these difficulties. For example, we
have been urged to use personal problems or personalized aspects of public problems to increase motivation. Other suggestions include a consideration of the
moral development of the student. In this regard,
because many workers report difficulty in making
students "sensitive to the arguments of other people," I would suggest role-switching exercises. Moreover, the device of introducing a research phase and a
desirability versus feasibility discussion—utilized by
Frank Simon of the University of Calgary, Canada
—has brought good results in increasing the level of
student involvement. Even simulation, in some cases,
is worthwhile. Some practitioners report rigidity
when personal emotions are involved. Yet, Ronald
Lippitt and I have found the use of small discussion
groups exceptionally helpful in inducing greater
openness. I have also used spacing, acting, role
switching, mode switching (shifting to a written report, possibly anonymous), and other techniques with
some success. The learner's tendency to make a game
out of beating others or the teacher, which other critics find depressing, I find challenging: a challenge to
rephrase the problem, or to select a more shocking
analogy, or to use another teacher or resource person
who is himself involved, or to find a movie or a novel
that sets a sharper edge.

Oliver and Bane also believe that there are presuppositions in the rational approach that their experience has shown to be invalid. They write:

> Society is seen as a compact of rational
> men . . . conflicts can be resolved without
> disrupting society in any fundamental way. . . .

There is a societal consensus on basic values . . .[4]

I mention these arguments because they typify a general attack on the merits of rationality.

But such case materials and methods, as opposed to some of the "meta-talk," are not really appropriate to the rational approach. They are not committed to reason any more than math courses are committed to the view that society is a compact of computers. In short, we may have a straw-man phenomenon, possibly unique in that the straw-man himself is a self-caricature.

What is the alternative? "The ability to see paradox and tragedy in human nature rather than consistence and universality in moral rules may be a more important part of 'the moral personality' than rational moral reasoning," write Oliver and Bane.[5] This may be so in fact; it may even be desirable. But it is in any case not exclusive of the other approach until trial and error have demonstrated otherwise.

We do, indeed, need a methodology for dealing with the affective dimension in moral education. But such a methodology cannot replace reason as a problem-solving device. Reasoning is, in this sense, never enough. It is always the slave of the passions, the instrument of man's prerational needs. That, in sum, is what it is for. We must not exaggerate its utility, but neither can we afford to discard it, or to suppose that it cannot influence its masters, the passions.

In addition, Oliver and Bane imply that "ritualistic celebration of metaphor," perhaps even theology, may be needed to express our humanity, and that it is

4. Oliver & Bane, *op. cit.*, p. 262.
5. Oliver & Bane, *op. cit.*, p. 261.

vital to acknowledge our humanity and to acknowledge our limitations and not exceed reality. Indeed so —but does not pure reason demand this? It is hardly turning away from reason to be realistic. Violence, to use one of their examples, may indeed be a necessity and not merely a means to an end. Such a possibility must be explored, for it would be unreasonable to act as if it did not exist, and it would be particularly unreasonable to teach as if it did not. Oliver and Bane distinguish angst and empathy, and the tragic from reason. I, in turn, point to the fact that they use reason to make their distinctions. We might say that the process of reasoning is not man's only interest or activity, but it is the only vehicle for investigating the existence and nature of other domains. Hence, reason is the basic tool, the knife of the mind.

The opponents of rationality emphasize the importance of multiple alternatives—in staff, modes of expression, and tasks. Their concept of pluralism, which parallels some of my own thinking, is a highly creative extension of the school into a community center characterized by work-study and play-study activities. The next century will surely see—at least, should surely see—such expressions.

They are also skeptical about the influence of training in developing moral reasoning. Oliver's own work is outstanding in the field, and his perceptions about the limitations of teaching should incline us toward remedies rather than pessimism. The needed improvement he notes can well be seen as rational extensions of training toward rationality. I suspect the rhetoric of antireason may pervade his conclusions and cloud his insights.

The critics maintain, moreover, that drama and ritual may be better ways to describe phenomena than the language of moral-social analysis, and that the traditional fields of ethics and social science may be less useful for the clarification of issues than other epistemological modalities. As supplements, yet. While the concepts of description and clarification are the business of logic and science, they do not fix the insights we derive from art and life. A full sense of the human condition does demand more than logic and science. But it is an error to think that the results will actually give us extra truths of the kind that logic and science deal with—namely, descriptions, classifications, propositions. In their place, there is no substitute for them. It makes good sense to argue for more than science in the curriculum, but not to upbraid reason that transcends science and clarifies its limitations—thus helping to reconcile the clashing claims of other visions and to extract the still, small voice of truth.

In the end the opposers of rationality arrive at several constructive suggestions. Reason leads them to a new curriculum, one with Bonnie and Clyde replacing Bonnie Prince Charlie, with new institutions—nonschools, wherein nonauthoritarian discussions, aesthetic explorations, and experimentation in communications can take place. We need the revolution within reason, not against it.

CONCLUSION

"The sign of the child's moral maturity," says L. Kohlberg, "is his ability to make moral judgments and formulate moral principles of his own rather than his ability to conform to moral judgments of the adults around him."[6]

6. L. Kohlberg, "Moral Education, Religious Education, and the Public Schools: A Developmental View," in Theodore Sizer, ed., *Religion and Public Education* (Boston: Houghton Mifflin, 1967), p. 179.

Maturity, autonomy, moral education—these themes are closely linked indeed. I hope they become the structure of our curriculum. They should at least be our credo in judging new curricula and methods— or anticurricula and antimethods. Religious tolerance nearly always finds itself strained when it has to embrace the atheist. So it is with the rationalist; he is interested in new rational methods but not in the rejection of reason. Maturity requires him to study the latter with greater care. That study is what I have been about here. For we do not yet need a requiem for reason.

editor's comments

SCRIVEN BEGINS with two admonitions. He reminds us that education's problems will not go away by themselves; there is no escape from the mounting problems that must be overcome. Secondly, he makes it clear that, in attempting to deal with these problems, we must distinguish between authentic change and fads, here and there, which come to no more than empty shibboleths. He is equally unwilling to champion an uncritical acceptance of the old —what he is after is a curriculum that can withstand the rigors of logic and reason.

He seeks a school that can deliver both a rational human being and a moral one. As does Meade in the earlier chapter, Scriven believes that schoolrooms are places where children ought to learn to select their values for themselves. "It is entirely immoral," he says, "to suppose we have any right to pass on values to other human beings, because passing on in this context means indoctrination." He opts, therefore, for an intellectually open school that permits "a free marketplace of ideas."

A pragmatic philosopher, he does not see schools as

preparation for later life. Rather, with Dewey, he sees the "now" experience—in school as well as out—as life itself. On this point, again, we find a striking concurrence with the previous chapter; it is these life experiences that, properly, ought to be the subject of the curriculum.

Scriven, however, has a special emphasis; "Reason," he tells us, "is the best route to truth." Rather than indoctrinate, we must forearm the student against all those forces in the society that seek to distribute prefabricated judgments. Rationality, in other words, is the purest fountainhead of values. Personal emotions may work to impede rationality, for reasoning is always the slave of the passions. Hence, while he is sensitive to the enormous influence of emotion, Scriven contends that affect cannot be allowed to dominate reason; he views the current cult of antireason as negative and destructive.

His anger is directed most forcefully against the school that exploits its constituents. Making a clear distinction between legitimate acculturation and socialization that in truth is deliberate depersonalization, Scriven calls upon the school to counterbalance the massive indoctrination that takes place outside its walls. Viewed in the aggregate, his arguments lend an impressive support to his position: we must strive for a mature school and a mature society; we must endeavor to make people sensitive to the valuable, as opposed to the novel; each generation must find its own value system in the conditions characteristic of its time; each generation must create a revolution from those that came before. Because rationality is the way to truth —that is, to true values—he argues, "We need the revolution within reason, not against it."

Scriven would unquestionably endorse Tyler's belief in the importance of autonomy, and Meade's faith in the value of confrontation. The real subject matter, he maintains, is the society itself. By probing life and subjecting it to rational analysis, the student comes to know himself and the world. More, in so doing, he also comes to know what is important and what is trivial. For Scriven, social revolutions are useful events that lead to new stability.

As editor, it would be presumptuous and perhaps even impudent of me to comment upon the difference of opinion between Scriven and Joseph Schwab and Donald Oliver, which Scriven explicates in the latter portion of the chapter. This notwithstanding, however, the issue at stake is a crucial one: when we act upon our emotions, do we of necessity deny our reason and act irrationally? In seeking an answer, obviously, it is technically far easier to examine children's reasoning than to attempt to plumb their psyches. This, in large measure, probably accounts for our reluctance to deal adequately with the latter. (It is this very reluctance, in point of fact, that gave rise to this volume.) The crux of the problem lies in a sane use of affect, and an intelligent fusion of logic and emotion in the curriculum. It is probable that Scriven, Oliver, Bane, Schwab, and Kohlberg all would agree that both have their place in schooling. The point of significance, therefore, is that of balance and perspective. With respect to this necessary coalescence, my own best hunch is that sometimes we choose to act on the basis of our emotions and sometimes on the basis of our reason. What is critical in this regard is not the action per se, but the recognition that the behavior is rationally or emotionally inspired, and the freedom of choice between the two modes. That is, the individual should be neither blindly emotional nor blindly rational.

"Maturity, autonomy, and moral education," Scriven concludes, are the chief things. They most probably represent our greatest need at the moment, precisely because they are among the most difficult to accomplish. But Scriven provides some clues for action—his curriculum, for example, would require the mass reeducation of parents; a reeducation that would enable them to prize, for their children, not their own values, but their children's right to fabricate a new and perhaps better system. It would require, as well, the presence of teachers who could avoid "exploiting" their students and teaching a "dogma from which comes no understanding." This is a tall order indeed, and perhaps an impossible one. To acquire roughly two million teachers, capable of setting aside their own attitudes and beliefs, their own conceptions of the good, true, and beautiful, is a Herculean task. Moreover, the development of maturity, autonomy, and morality are lofty ideals, difficult to organize into a learning matrix. This is not to say, however, that we ought not to try; for even minimal success would provide a massive step forward.

5.

If we wish, we can virtually guarantee that all children will master whatever lessons we choose to teach. The cost is high, perhaps prohibitively so. Nonetheless, the forthcoming reform must deal with the true meaning of equal educational opportunity.

chapter 5

INDIVIDUAL DIFFERENCES IN SCHOOL ACHIEVE-MENT: A VANISHING POINT?

•

Benjamin S. Bloom

EDITOR'S PREFACE

An argument could be made that the most damaging flaw of the present educational system is located inside the teacher's head. Each teacher begins a new course or term with the expectation that about one-third of his students will adequately learn what he has to teach. He also expects about one-third of his students to learn a good deal of what he was to teach, but not enough to be regarded as good students, and another one-third to fail or to just "get by." Supported by school policies and practices in grading, this set of expectations becomes transmitted not only through the grading procedures but also through the methods and materials of instruction as well. The school system creates a self-fulfilling prophecy such that the final sorting of students through the grading process becomes approximately equivalent to these expectations.

This set of expectations reduces the aspirations of both teachers and students; it reduces motivation for learning in students; and it systematically destroys the egos and self-confidence of a sizable group of students who are legally required to attend school for ten to twelve years under conditions that are continually frustrating and humiliating.

The normal curve for grading students implicit in this set of expectations has been used for so long that we have come to believe in it. Our achievement measures are designed to detect differences among our students, even if the differences are trivial in terms of the subject matter. We then distribute our grades according to this normal curve, expecting in any group of students to have some small percent (usually about 10 percent) receive A grades. We also expect about an equal proportion of students to fail. Quite frequently these failures are determined by the rank order of the students in the group rather than by their inability to grasp the essential ideas of the course. It does not seem to matter that the failures of one year performed at about the same level as the C students of another year, or that the A students of one school perform about as well as the F students of another school. We have become accustomed to classifying students into about five categories or levels of performance and then to assigning grades accordingly.

Having become conditioned to this normal

distribution, we set grade policies in these terms and are dismayed when some teacher recommends a different distribution. A teacher whose grade distribution is normal, rather than different, will avoid difficulties with administrators, who are constantly on the alert to control teachers who are "too easy" or "too hard" in their grading. But even more important, through this grading system and also by our system of quiz and progress testing we convince many, if not most, students that they can do only C or D or failing work. Finally, we proceed in our teaching as though only the minority of our students should be able to learn what we have to teach. It seems clear that the costs of this system, in reducing opportunities for further learning and in alienating youth from both school and society, are so great that no society can tolerate them for long.

In his now celebrated work on mastery learning, Benjamin Bloom discussed the basic argument. In this, the present essay, he turns his attention to some of the secondary implications of these earlier findings.

Bloom's principal point in this essay is that no society need tolerate indefinitely the practice or results of normal-curve distribution of student achievement. While there is great inertia behind the idea that some students have the aptitude to learn certain subjects and others do not, recent research is challenging that formerly unchallengeable part of American educational folklore. Implicit in this formulation is the assumption that given enough time all students can conceivably attain mastery of a learning task. The fundamental idea underlying Mastery Learning, which is discussed in the following essay, is that all students, or nearly all students, can learn any given subject. The "normal" distribution of achievement is artificial, unnecessary, and represents considerable social and individual loss. If student aptitude for a subject is distributably normal, but we give each student the time he needs to learn, the help he needs to learn, and the encouragement he needs to learn, then Bloom's theory is that the distribution of achievement will not be normal, that 90 percent or more of the students will do as well as the top 10 percent would do under normal conditions, and that the correlation between aptitude and achievement should come close to zero.

We must hope for a development in American social values that respects the belief that one's sense of adequacy might derive from handling problems rather than from besting one's peers. It is possible that the full advantages of Mastery Learning will only be realizable in a society with somewhat different values than those that currently exist in America, values that place a higher premium upon cooperation and upon each human's right to realize his potential. One is tempted to suggest that the acceptance of an educational theory stressing the fullest achievement for all, even at considerable additional social costs in time and effort, may be one index of the progress of democratic social change in America.

FOUR YEARS AGO I had the opportunity of presenting some ideas about education and learning under the title, "Learning for Mastery".[1] In the intervening time, I have been surprised by the extent to which these ideas have been applied in the schools. And, I have been delighted with the quality of the research studies that deal with some of the underlying issues and hypotheses in my paper.

The findings of these applied as well as more basic research studies have been summarized in a book, *Mastery Learning* by James Block[2]. He has brought together the results of about forty studies in the schools in the United States and abroad. These studies are at various levels of education from the elementary school through the graduate and professional schools. They also cover a great variety of courses and subject fields. It is of interest to note that not all of the investigators in the applied studies were aware that they were using mastery approaches. Like the users of prose, some of them had to be convinced by Block that what they were doing was defined as mastery learning.

While mastery learning strategies have not all been successful, those that were reported in the published literature or in some other written form were generally quite effective. I had estimated that under ideal conditions up to 95 percent of students could achieve mastery in a particular subject. Only a few of the reported studies have reached this level. In the majority of studies, about 75 percent of students under mastery learning strategies reach levels of achievement attained by the top 20 percent of students under

1. *Benjamin S. Bloom, "Learning for Mastery," University of California Evaluation Comment* (Los Angeles: Center for the Study of Evaluation, UCLA 1968), Vol. I, #2.
2. James H. Block, *Mastery Learning: Theory and Practice* (New York: Holt, Rinehart and Winston, 1971).

control conditions. Also there is virtual elimination of failing performances.

There are many different possible approaches to mastery learning. Perhaps what they all have in common is the attempt to produce under group conditions (a teacher with thirty or more learners) some of the features of teaching and learning that might be produced with an ideal tutor working with a single student. They have in common, also, the attempt to help each student reach a criterion level on each learning unit or section of a course as a prelude to reaching the criterion level of performance on one or more summative evaluation instruments.

But I really do not wish here to discuss mastery learning per se. Mastery learning strategies do work —not as well as I believe theoretically possible, but better than I had a right to expect in view of my long and sometimes frustrating experiences with education in the schools. What I do want to present are some of the problems, conceptions, and speculations arising from our work on mastery learning. Also, I want to present mastery learning strategies not as a means of reaching a given criterion of achievement but as a set of research tools and concepts for educational research in school settings. My main focus here is on individual differences in school achievement—their prediction, control, and modification.

A LEARNING UNIT

In John Carroll's "A Model of School Learning"[3] and in the mastery learning strategies derived from this work, it is necessary to relate the learning and teaching to a smaller unit than an entire course or

3. John Carroll, "A Model of School Learning," *Teachers College Record* 64 (1963): 723-33.

curriculum. This basic unit may be a learning activity, a learning project, a learning task, or some other way of conceiving of an interaction between a *learner, something to be learned,* and a *teacher* or mentor.

In much of our work we have regarded the basic unit of learning as a learning task. We have given much thought to the problem of defining a learning task and have come to regard it as something to be learned over a period of a few hours of instruction—perhaps something between a single hour and ten hours. But, more fundamental is that the learning task involves a whole that consists of elements or details to be learned in some arrangement. In mastery learning applied in school settings, we have found it convenient to consider the learning task as a chapter, section, or unit that is part of a series of such learning tasks.

We have found it possible to provide techniques of definition and classification such that two or more experts can independently identify the elements to be learned in a task with over 90 percent agreement. Such experts can also identify the interrelationships among the elements with about 85 percent agreement. We have been able to develop formative evaluation instruments that have high content validity and which satisfactorily reproduce the hypothesized interrelationships among the elements. In general, the construct validity of the formative tests is rarely as high as we desire when studied under actual teaching-learning conditions, but about three-fourths of the item responses are in the hypothesized patterns.

Thus, we regard the learning task as a fundamental unit that can be analyzed, evaluated, taught, and learned. Such a unit may be cognitive, psychomotor, or even largely affective in nature. However, our main experience to date is primarily with cognitive tasks. Such tasks may be relatively simple types of knowledge tasks or they may be very complex and require higher level objectives and complex hierarchical arrangements of elements. A learning task for educational purposes should not be confused with simple training tasks, although one does not necessarily exclude the other.

While the learning task is the basic unit with which we have been working in mastery learning strategies and related research studies, of fundamental importance in education is that learning tasks are organized in the schools in some arrangement. The arrangement of learning tasks may be in a tight sequential series in which mastery of one task is required as a prerequisite to another task. The arrangement may also be only a preferred order in which each task is independent of other tasks such that they could really be learned in a random order. In this presentation, I will concern myself primarily with the former class of tasks—that is those in which there is a relatively tight sequential arrangement and where the sequence of learning tasks is a necessary one for a particular set of instructional and logical purposes. However, I must hasten to point out that such an arrangement is necessary only because the particular curriculum and instructional material has been set in this fashion—and not because of some God-given mandate about the necessary arrangement or because of some natural or learning theory requirement. Nevertheless, I am of the opinion that over one-half of the curriculum in the public schools consists of learning tasks in a sequential arrangement.

LABORATORY VS. SCHOOL LEARNING

I wish to distinguish between the usual psychological laboratory experimentation on learning and the actual conditions of learning in the schools. Much of learning experimentation in psychological laboratory research is concerned with a single learning task. In such research, it is usually found that most of the learners (animal or human) can attain the criterion of mastery set by the experimenter, although some learners will reach the criterion in a minimum number of trials or amount of time while others may need a much larger number of trials or greater amount of time. Thus, all or most of the learners will reach the criterion although time and/or trials will vary. Individual differences are thus exemplified in the amount of time or number of trials to reach the criterion level of performance. It is this common observation in psychological research that led us to the view that most students could reach mastery learning criteria, although different learners would need different amounts of time (or help) to reach the criterion. This amounted to little more than a shift from observing individual variations in achievement levels when all learners are given equal time or similar instructional conditions to one of having most learners reach a criterion level with individual variations in the amount of time or help to reach the criterion.

Quite in contrast to psychological learning research emphasizing a single learning task are the actual conditions in schools where students are expected to learn a sequence of learning tasks over a semester, year, or even over a number of years. In the schools, the *history* of the learner with regard to the early learning in the sequence is of fundamental importance to his learning of the tasks in later portions of the sequence. Thus, a basic difference between studies of learning in psychological laboratories and the study of learning in school settings is that the history of the learners is largely controlled or ignored in the former while it is of the essence in the latter. In addition, group learning is the general case for school learning throughout the world, while psychological studies of learning characteristically deal with one learner at a time. These, as well as other differences in the two types of situations, make it likely that psychological laboratory studies of learning will lead to one type of learning theory, while quite another view or theory of learning is required to account for the learning in school settings.

INDIVIDUAL VARIATION

Individual variation in learning is the observed phenomenon in almost all classrooms, schools, or educational programs. Student variation is almost invariably found in either the *level of learning* as measured by a set of achievement tests or in the *rate of learning* if all students are expected to reach a criterion level on the summative measures.

This is the common observation, and I am sure each reader can testify that there are great individual differences in achievement in his own classes. Therefore, why should anyone propose the farfetched notion that individual differences in achievement can be eliminated (or at least significantly reduced) and that individual differences in school achievement are artifacts of our approach to schooling and group learning conditions rather than the "normal" variations that are derived from fundamental variations in the nature of man and his characteristics. The subtitle of this chapter asks the question, Can individual differences in school achievement reach the vanishing point? Is there such a vanishing point or is this as much an illusion in education as it is in visual perception? Let me begin by stating that the vanishing point in individual variation in school achievement is as rare as the perfect vacuum on the face of the earth. But, with sufficient care and effort we can approach a vanishing point in individual variation in school achievement just as we can create an almost perfect vacuum, if it is worth the time, effort, and costs required. That it is theoretically and practicably possible in both cases does not necessarily make it worth the investment and care required. The justification must come from other considerations.

ACHIEVEMENT VARIATION IN SCHOOL SETTINGS

In Chart 1, I have indicated three possible sets of distributions of school achievement in the elementary grades. Set A shows what we typically observe in a subject such as reading or arithmetic. At the end of the first grade there is considerable variation in the distribution of achievement. This variation increases each year until by the end of grade six it may be approximately doubled. While some of this increased variation may be ascribed to the nature of the measurements and to the increased precision of achievement measurement in the higher grades, few would doubt that increased variation in student achievement is a real phenomenon that will not go away merely by improving our measurements.

Quite in contrast to the first set is a theoretical set of curves, Set B, in which the variation in achieve-

CHART 1

Some Possible Distributions of School Achievement

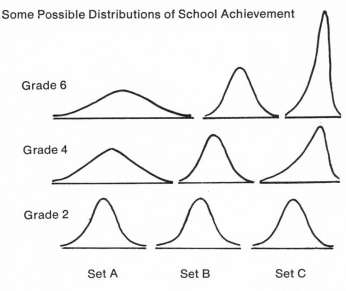

Grade 6

Grade 4

Grade 2

Set A   Set B   Set C

ment remains constant from grade to grade. I believe a few schools or classes may be found with results like this, but I imagine these would be rare instances. Such curves might be expected if there is considerable stability of general intelligence and other relevant aptitudes during the years six to twelve, and if the schools or homes do a good job of helping individual learners whenever they encounter special difficulties in learning. I believe such curves would not be too difficult to produce, if a school staff deliberately sought to achieve the student learning suggested by them.

But the third set, Set C, in which the variation decreases each year until by the sixth grade it is only about 10 percent of the variation in the first grade, is something that I doubt that any teacher has ever encountered. And yet, this is precisely the change in distributions that I believe is possible both theoretically and practicably. While I must confess that we have not produced curves like these over a six-year school period, studies of mastery learning classes and control classes in particular courses or subjects yield curves over a semester or year like Sets A and C. That is, for increasing variation in achievement over time in the control classes and, in contrast, decreasing variation over time in the mastery learning classes.

How is this accomplished in a single course and what are the underlying variables that account for such vastly different pictures of student achievement?

In Chart 2, I have sketched a sequence of ten learning units. Think of these as the chapters or units in a course such as arithmetic, algebra, physics, chemistry, or even a second language. Think of these as a highly sequential set of units such that Unit 5 could not be learned before Units 2 or 3, while a high level of competence in Unit 1 is required if Unit 2 is to be learned adequately, and so on throughout the sequence. Assume also that if a student does not learn a unit adequately at the time it is taught, he cannot learn (or relearn) it at a later time.

Now, under Condition A, let us assume that 90 percent of the students learn Unit 1 adequately, while 10 percent do not. Under the assumptions I have indicated in the foregoing paragraph, these 10 percent will not learn any of the later units (2 to 10) adequately, because Unit 1 is basic to all that follows. Let us assume that while 90 percent of the students learned Unit 1 adequately some of these will not learn Unit 2 adequately. Similarly, for each additional unit, we will assume that additional students fall by the wayside until by Unit 10 only 10 percent learn it adequately while 90 percent do not. If we

CHART 2

Student Achievement under Two Conditions

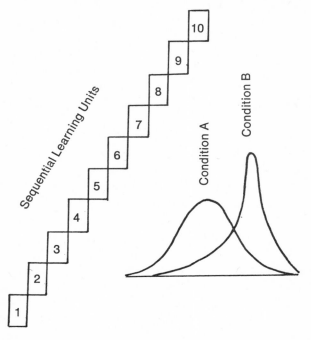

then give a summative test in which all ten units are equally represented, the curve of achievement is likely to approximate a normal distribution with considerable individual variation.

Under Condition B, let us also assume that 90 percent of the students learn Unit 1 adequately (or to a level of mastery) while 10 percent do not. But under Condition B, these 10 percent are then helped (outside of class time) until at least 5 percent or more have achieved mastery. The proportion who achieve mastery of Unit 1 will now reach 95 percent (the original 90 percent plus the additional 5 percent) before they enter Unit 2. Assume that this process is repeated on each unit and the goal is always to have 95 percent of the students achieve mastery on a unit before embarking on the next unit in the sequence. Using the same summative examination as in Condition A, we should find that over 90 percent of the students under Condition B reach about the same level of achievement as the top 10 percent of the students under Condition A. The two distributions will be roughly as indicated in Chart 2. So much for two theoretical distributions. One resembles Curve A at grade six in Chart 1 while the other resembles Curve C at grade six in the same chart.

But what has been especially exciting in some of our research on mastery learning is the shift in the amount of time and help required at each of the units in our course. On Unit 1 we are likely to find that some of the students reach mastery in 1X amount of time and help while other students reach this same level of achievement only after as much as 10X amounts of time and help. Perhaps, by the sixth task, the variation may be from 1X to 4X. By the tenth unit, if all has gone well, the variation in time and help required may only be from 1X to 2X.

Thus, in a sequential series of learning tasks, the students (under mastery learning conditions) are likely to become more and more similar in the amounts of time and help they require to reach a given criterion of achievement. What we have done is to maintain a given criterion of achievement but varied the amount of time and help needed to achieve it. In turn, the variation in time and help required gradually moves toward a vanishing point. But let me remind you that we never did reach the *vanishing point,* although we have observed situations in which the variation in time and help required on the later units was only 10 percent of the variation observed in the first learning task (or unit) in the sequential series. I commend this type of teaching-learning situation to you and hope that you, too, find situations in which the crutch of additional time and help is gradually discarded until most of the students learn easily without the need of such learning aids. But let me assure you that it is more common to find situations in which mastery learning approaches succeed in bringing the students to a given criterion level of achievement, even if one cannot eliminate most of the variation in time and help required.

But to return to our idealized (and occasionally observed) situation of mastery with less and less variation in time and help required. Why should (or does) it work? What have we been doing? What are the underlying variables we have been manipulating in our sequential learning situations? I believe there are three types of variables that account for the major differences between Conditions A and B in Chart 2. These variables should be useful in understanding the conditions under which individual differences in school achievement are likely to be maximized and they can help us create conditions under which individual differences in achievement can be minimized.

ENTRY BEHAVIOR

Education and learning in the schools are built on sets of prior learnings, largely cognitive in nature. For each learning task there are some prerequisite learnings that are required if the student is to attain mastery of the task. We have chosen to call these prerequisite learnings *entry behaviors*.[4] We believe it

---

4. Robert Glaser, "Evaluation of Instruction and Changing Education Models," *The Evaluation of Instruction,* ed. M.C. Wittrock and D.E. Wiley (New York: Holt, Rinehart and Winston, 1970).

possible to construct test instruments to determine the extent to which students possess these prerequisite behaviors and we have been attempting to determine psychometric techniques to establish the extent to which hypothesized entry behaviors are necessary (or unnecessary) for the learning of a specific task.

We believe it is impossible for a learner to achieve mastery on a learning task if he does not possess the essential entry behaviors for it. However, it is sometimes possible to alter a learning task in a number of ways so that each alteration requires different entry behaviors. Under such conditions, a student who lacks one set of entry behaviors but possesses another relevant set may learn the task to mastery.

In Chart 2, Condition A, the reason for students failing each learning task was in part the lack of the prerequisite entry behaviors (largely developed in the prior learning tasks). The reason for students becoming both successful and more efficient in their learning over Units 2 to 10 under Condition B was that they were acquiring the prerequisite entry behaviors before entering the subsequent learning tasks. Note that the determination of the entry behaviors required is a much more complex problem for Unit 1 than for the subsequent units, because Unit 1 becomes (by definition) the prerequisite for Unit 2, and Unit 2 for Unit 3, and so forth. That is, the problem of defining and evaluating entry behaviors is more difficult for the beginning of a sequential series of learning tasks than it is for learning tasks within a series.

We have reviewed a large number of longitudinal and predictive studies of learning achievement and have come to the tentative conclusion that variation in entry behaviors can account for up to 50 percent of the variation in achievement on one or more learning tasks.

CHART 3

Estimated Effect of Selected Variables
on Variation in School Achievement

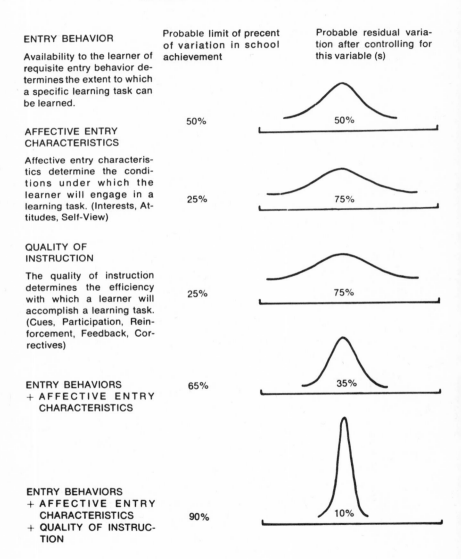

	Probable limit of precent of variation in school achievement	Probable residual variation after controlling for this variable (s)
ENTRY BEHAVIOR Availability to the learner of requisite entry behavior determines the extent to which a specific learning task can be learned.	50%	50%
AFFECTIVE ENTRY CHARACTERISTICS Affective entry characteristics determine the conditions under which the learner will engage in a learning task. (Interests, Attitudes, Self-View)	25%	75%
QUALITY OF INSTRUCTION The quality of instruction determines the efficiency with which a learner will accomplish a learning task. (Cues, Participation, Reinforcement, Feedback, Correctives)	25%	75%
ENTRY BEHAVIORS + AFFECTIVE ENTRY CHARACTERISTICS	65%	35%
ENTRY BEHAVIORS + AFFECTIVE ENTRY CHARACTERISTICS + QUALITY OF INSTRUCTION	90%	10%

In Chart 3 we have suggested that if all the learners in a learning task are equal in possession of the necessary entry behaviors, the achievement of the group would show only about 50 percent of the variation of a group that varies widely in the possession of the necessary entry behaviors. One can demonstrate this in learning studies by selecting students who possess the necessary entry behaviors, by statistical control procedures, or by actually teaching the students the necessary entry behaviors before they proceed to the particular learning task.

In this connection, we have speculated that general intelligence tests, aptitude tests, and other predictors will predict achievement on a learning task to the extent to which they include indices of the relevant entry behaviors. That is, our scholastic aptitude tests do predict because they are useful general indicators of the relevant entry behaviors. However, rarely will they be as predictive of achievement (or as useful in understanding learning and learning difficulties) as more direct indicators of the relevant entry behaviors.

Space does not allow going on in greater detail about the many hypotheses for research and the implications for educational practice relating to entry behaviors. The ideas are really not new—perhaps what is novel is our attempt to do something about them in terms of evaluation, research, and practice.

AFFECTIVE ENTRY CHARACTERISTICS

Motivation to attempt a new learning task is in part determined by the individual's perception of his success or failure with previous learning tasks that he believes to be similar or related. Such motivation is largely predicated on the student's belief that the new learning task is in some way related to previous learning tasks he has encountered. It is the student's perception of his history with related learning tasks that is of importance—even though the new task may be in no way related to previous learning tasks he has experienced. Over a period of time, the learner acquires relatively fixed notions about his competence with such learning tasks and these determine the efforts he will make, the degree of confidence he has in the effectiveness of his efforts, and what he will do when he encounters difficulties or obstacles in the learning.

We regard the affective entry characteristics as a compound of interests and attitudes toward the subject matter of the learning task, attitudes toward the school and schooling, and more deep-seated self-concepts and personality characteristics. Some of these components may be highly changeable while others may be relatively stable—this is in part a function of age and previous experiences. While it is not impossible for a learner to achieve mastery on a learning task if he has negative affective entry characteristics, it is very difficult. We believe that it is sometimes possible to present a learning task so that the student will regard it as independent of previous learning tasks and may approach it with positive or even neutral affect. Operationally, what is sought is an openness to the new learning task, a willingness to make the effort required, and sufficient confidence in the self to strive to overcome real or imagined obstacles in the learning.

In Chart 2, Condition A, the reason for students failing each learning task was in part the creation of negative affective entry characteristics by failure or at least the lack of clear success on the previous learning tasks. Under Condition B, students were acquiring positive affect before entering subsequent learning tasks. Note again that the determination of affective entry characteristics is a more complex problem for Unit 1 than it is for subsequent units in the sequence.

We have reviewed a large number of studies of interests, attitudes, self-concept, and more general studies of motivation as related to school learning. On the basis of this review, we have come to the tentative conclusion that the affective entry characteristics can account for up to 25 percent of the variation in achievement on one or more learning tasks.

In Chart 3 we have suggested that if all the learners in a learning task are similar in possession of positive affective entry characteristics that the achievement of the group would show about 75 percent of the variation of a group that varies widely with regard to such characteristics.

Because affective entry characteristics are usually found to be related to cognitive entry behavior, our best general estimate of the combined effect of both cognitive and affective entry characteristics is represented by a multiple correlation of about +.80 (see Chart 3)—that is, up to two-thirds of the variance on achievement measures can be accounted for by the combined effects of these entry characteristics. Some support for this estimate comes from longitudinal studies of grades and other achievement measures within a school, where previous achievement indexes correlate about +.80 with achievement in the same subject over the next semester or year. We regard previous achievement indexes as combinations of cognitive and affective entry characteristics.

One striking phenomenon we have noted about affective entry characteristics is that they are primarily within-school variables. That is, the student typically gains his perceptions about how well he is doing from his position within a group of his peers. He also gets most of the feedback on his success from the teacher and local evaluations, rather than from national standardized achievement tests. It is thus possible to find two schools with minimal overlap on standardized achievement test distributions where the top students in the lower school have highly positive affective entry characteristics, while the bottom students in the higher school have very negative affective entry characteristics—even though the two groups may be very similar in their scores on the standardized achievement test. The main point to note is that affective characteristics are largely perceptual phenomena arising from the student's perception of how well he is learning and that this is usually based on the evidence and judgments he receives from the teachers, parents, and his peers in the school or class.

QUALITY OF INSTRUCTION

In spite of the many pessimistic notes about the lack of measurable effects of the teacher or school on learning (largely derived from large-scale survey and evaluation projects), we are of the view that the quality of instruction students receive has a demonstrable effect on their achievement over one or more learning tasks.

Our problem has been to make more explicit just what it is that constitutes poor or good quality of instruction. We have found it difficult to gain much insight about this process by observing a teacher teaching a group of thirty or more learners, because the teacher appears to spend so much of his effort in managing the students rather than on managing the learning.

One approach to determining the specific aspects of quality of instruction may be derived from observing a very good tutor attempting to teach something to one student. What is the interaction that appears to promote the learning of this one student?

Perhaps the clearest subvariable in quality of instruction has to do with the cues that the tutor uses to make clear what is to be learned, what the student is to do, and how he is to do it. We observe that the tutor uses a variety of ways of explaining, illustrating, demonstrating, and so forth, what is to be learned. And, the good tutor adapts or alters the cues to present those that work best for the particular learner. For some students, the cues can be derived from written materials, for others it may be oral explanations, for others it may be combinations of demonstrations or models with explanations, and so forth. This aspect of quality of instruction is similar to Carroll's model in which he defines quality of instruction as the degree to which the presentation, explanation, and ordering of the elements of the task to be learned approach the optimum for a given learner.

A second aspect of quality of instruction is the extent to which it gets the learner in active participation or practice of the responses to be learned. While some of this participation may be overt and observable by the tutor, it is also likely that covert participation may be as effective in some situations as the more overt or observable participation. The good tutor has little trouble in observing the active participation of the learner in the process. Furthermore, he recognizes that there may be individual differences in the amount of practice or participation needed and he can easily secure enough evidence to determine when the individual student has practiced sufficiently.

Finally, the good tutor uses reinforcement (positive

or negative) at various stages in the learning process. The tutor adapts his reinforcers to the learner. What is an excellent reward for one student may not operate in the same way for another student. The tutor uses a variety of reinforcers (both extrinsic and intrinsic), he adapts them to the needs of the learner, and he provides them to the learner as frequently as they are needed and at the points in the learning process where they are most effective.

These three aspects of quality of instruction (cues, participation, reinforcement) may be observed with little difficulty in an effective tutor-student interaction. These three may be derived from such theories of learning as J. Dollard and N.E. Miller[5] and, although the terms may differ, they can be found in some respect in almost every theory of learning as summarized by E.R. Hilgard.[6]

But so far we have been approaching the problem of quality of instruction as though we had an ideal tutor with one learner. This is a far cry from the teaching under group conditions with thirty or more learners in the typical school classroom. While cues, participation, and reinforcement are necessary in both individual and group learning situations, there are quantitative as well as qualitative differences in the two situations. We note in the tutor-learner situation that the tutor constantly adapts to the individual learner on the basis of a great deal of immediate evidence he is receiving from the learner in the learning process. In the group situation, the very skillful teacher may develop a variety of techniques for managing the instruction and for adapting to the varying

5. John Dollard and N. E. Miller, *Personality and Psychotherapy* (New York: McGraw-Hill, 1950).
6. E. R. Hilgard, *Theories of Learning* (New York: Appleton-Century-Crofts, 1956).

needs and requirements of the different learners in the situation.

What is needed by all teachers in group learning situations is feedback evidence on the effectiveness of the learning process for individual students. Teachers also need to make relatively rapid use of corrective procedures when and where they are needed. Where mastery learning has been effective, it has made use of relatively explicit formative evaluation procedures to determine what the student has learned as well as what he still needs to learn before proceeding onto the next learning task in the sequence. Furthermore, through the use of a variety of instructional materials, through the use of students helping each other, or through the use of tutors and aides, it has been possible to quickly apply correctives with regard to cues, participation, and reinforcement when and where the learners are having difficulty in the learning process.

In Condition A in Chart 2, the main reason for students having increasing difficulty as they proceed from Unit 1 to Unit 10, is that nothing is done to correct inadequacies in the learning as they are encountered by the different students. In contrast, in Condition B there are formative evaluations accompanied by correctives for each learning task before the students proceed to the next learning unit.

Some evidence in support of different aspects of quality of instruction may be derived from the work of B.S.M. Anthony,[7] Block,[8] H.M. Lahaderne,[9] and

---

7. B.S.M. Anthony, "The Identification and Measurement of Classroom Environmental Process Variables Related to Academic Achievement," (Ph.D. diss., University of Chicago, 1967).

8. Block, *Mastery Learning: Theory and Practice.*

9. H.M. Lahaderne, "Adaptations to School Settings: A Study of Children's Attitudes and Classroom Behavior," (Ph.D. diss., University of Chicago, 1967).

B. Rosenshine.[10] In selected studies in the literature, the combination of several of these qualities of instruction account for 20 percent to 25 percent of the variation in achievement. In contrast to these studies of the interactive processes in the classroom are the many studies of teacher characteristics that rarely account for more than 10 percent of the variation in achievement.

From a review of these studies of the interactive processes in the classroom, it appears that the quality of instruction could account for up to 25 percent of the variation in achievement (see Chart 3). Because the quality of instruction cannot be predicted from the teacher's experience, education, or other characteristics, it is difficult for administrators to assign students to teachers who will provide high or low quality of instruction. Thus, it is likely that under such conditions the quality of instruction will be relatively independent of the student's characteristics. When entry behavior, affective entry characteristics, and quality of instruction are combined, they should account for up to 90 percent of the variation in *level of achievement* or in the *rate of achievement*.

Undoubtedly, these three major variables do not account for all the sources of variation in achievement, but they do indicate that when properly controlled, the variation in achievement still to be accounted for may only be about one-tenth of the original variation in student achievement. Thus, while variation in achievement does not reach the vanishing point, these theoretical and practical considerations do account for sufficient variation in the learning of a task or a series of learning tasks to en-

10. Barak Rosenshine, "Teaching Behaviors and Student Achievement: A Review of Research," (International Association for the Evaluation of Educational Achievement, Stockholm, 1970).

able us to hope that the control and manipulation of these major variables in the school learning processes will, in the present decade, enable us to improve the effectiveness of the schools by a significant degree.

It is left for future workers to more and more approximate a vanishing point in individual variation in school achievement.

But is all this only one more theoretical exercise in academic prediction and control? We can predict academic achievement with considerable success. And we can manipulate student and instructional variables to either maximize student variation or minimize it—if we decide that one is to be preferred to the other.

Each of my readers may have a point of view on which is to be preferred and why. I hope each of you will be provoked to give further thought to these problems in your research and in your work as a teacher, administrator, or scholar. What are the implications of these ideas for education and for our views of human nature and the human condition? Each of you will answer this question in your own way. One set of implications that some of us have been considering has to do with the affective consequences of school achievement. I will present them briefly.

AFFECTIVE CONSEQUENCES
OF SCHOOL ACHIEVEMENT

Mastery learning may be regarded as good if we (and the students) are convinced that there is any point to the mastering of the learning tasks and the educational objectives and content represented by them. Not all that we attempt to teach our students seems to be worth the effort. What is worth learning and what is worth learning well are questions we will have to face more clearly in the years ahead. And these questions can no longer be answered in the abstract, they must be asked and answered in relation to individual students and in relation to rapidly changing conceptions about the nature of knowledge, the nature of society, and the nature of man and the good life. The curriculum questions and the larger educational questions are not answered by a theory of how students may learn and how teachers may teach more effectively.

These are the questions that relate to the explicit curriculum of the schools and other educational agencies and processes. This curriculum may be of importance to the learners and to the society because of the competence it develops, because of the interests and attitudes it encourages, and because of the career opportunities and life-styles available to those who learn it well. The explicit curriculum is visible; it can be documented in many ways; and most of the resources and personnel of the schools are dedicated to the students' learning of some variations of this curriculum.

However, there is a second curriculum that is not so clearly visible. This is the implicit curriculum that is now experienced and learned differently by each student. This is the curriculum that teaches each student who he is in relation to others. It may also teach each student his place in the world of people, ideas, and activities. While the student may learn this curriculum more slowly than the other, it is likely that he will not be able to forget it as easily as he can forget the details of history, the rules of grammar, or the specifics of any subject of study in the explicit curriculum.

One aspect of the implicit curriculum is the effect

of evidence of repeated success or failure in the learning tasks on the student. Repeated evidence of success in a particular set of learning tasks is likely to
increase a student's confidence in himself with this
type of task and increase his interest in further learning tasks of this type. Repeated evidence of failure or
inadequacy in a set of learning tasks is likely to decrease the student's interest in further learning tasks
of this type. Such evidence of failure or inadequacy is
effective in narrowing the range of alternatives open
to the individual in school as well as in career and
life-style.

Repeated evidence of success or failure in a large
variety of learning tasks over a number of years is
likely to result in a generally favorable or unfavor-
able attitude toward school and school learning. Such
attitudes generalize from a particular set or range of
learning tasks to the entire institution of the school,
to most of the school subjects, to the staff of the
school, and even to the other students who attend the
school. Especially in the case of negative attitudes
toward school and school learning, these can have
consequences for all later efforts to do school learning or learning that is in any way related to schools.

For both interests and attitudes, the object of the
affect is outside the individual. The student develops
a disinterest in something or he develops an interest
in something. He develops a positive attitude toward
school and school learning or he develops a negative
attitude. While there is a difference in generality between interests and attitudes as we have defined
them, in both the object of affect is external to the individual.

If this process of adequate or inadequate apprais-
als with regard to learning tasks is generalized over a
large number of tasks over a number of years, even-

tually the object of appraisal for the student becomes shifted from the school subjects or the school to the self.

Successful experiences in school are no guarantee of a generally positive self-concept but they increase the probabilities that such will be the case. In contrast, unsuccessful experiences in school guarantee that the individual will develop a negative academic self-concept and increase the probabilities that he will have a generally negative self-concept. The individual strives desperately to secure some assurance of his self-worth and if he is denied it in one area he will search for it elsewhere. The likelihood of his finding it is considerably decreased by lack of success in the school.

There is considerable empirical support for relating the individual's perception of his adequacy in school learning to the development of related interests, attitudes, and self-concept. While we must be speculative on this point, we regard continual evidence of success or failure in the school as having major effects on the individual's personality and mental health. If the school environment provides the individual with evidence of his adequacy over a number of years and especially in the first six years, there is some evidence that this provides a type of immunization against mental illness for an indefinite period of time. Such an individual should be able to surmount crises and periods of great stress without suffering too much. His own sense of adequacy and his personal and technical skills should enable him to use realistic methods in surmounting these crises situations. We believe this should characterize a sizable proportion of students who are generally in the upper third of their classes on measures of achievement.

At the other extreme are students who have been

INDIVIDUAL DIFFERENCES IN ACHIEVEMENT 143

given consistent evidence of their inadequacy in the school learning environment over a similar period of time. Such students rarely secure any positive reinforcement in the classroom. We believe that such students are likely to be infected with emotional difficulties arising from the rarity with which they can secure any sense of adequacy in the school environment and especially in the classroom. Again, we believe this should characterize a sizeable proportion of students who are generally in the bottom third of their classes in grades and other measures of achievement.

In spite of the speculative nature of these ideas, there is theoretical support as well as clinical evidence for them. The extreme importance of this area for the individual and the society make it imperative that these speculations and hypotheses be the subject of more definitive research.

In closing, it is likely that student variation in achievement can be maximized or minimized by the appropriate use of the variables and school conditions I have discussed in this all too brief presentation. We are thus faced with new decisions that cannot be settled on the basis of personal preference and taste. In part, justification and support for these new decisions may be derived from an analysis of the relations between the individual and the explicit curriculum and from analyses of the relations between the individual and the implicit curriculum.

editor's comments

BLOOM'S RESEARCH is almost awesome in its implications. His outstanding contribution lies in the fact that, through painstaking and rigorous investigations, he has confirmed what many of us could only suspect. He has demonstrated, in short, that although children differ widely in their abilities, we can—by controlling the classroom events—guarantee that the vast majority will master any lesson we wish to teach. It is significant, I believe, that in this regard Bloom lets his findings speak—eloquently—for themselves. He has demonstrated that individual difference in school achievement can largely be made to vanish; we must decide for ourselves whether such an accomplishment is worth the effort.

Defining a learning task as "something to be learned over a period of a few hours of instruction," and "a fundamental unit that can be analysed, evaluated, taught, and learned," he makes it clear that such learning tasks may be cognitive, psychomotor, or affective. It is thus made obvious for us that a teaching goal can be directed toward any one, or any combination, of the three. Bloom's findings with respect to the importance of student attitudes suggest, moreover, that affect has a powerful bearing upon cognitive achievement.

We are treated, in this connection, to a related insight: much of our difficulty in applying research theory stemming from laboratory experiments on learning arises from the fact that such experiments have generally ignored those affective characteristics of the student, which have been conditioned over the course of his school history.

Another finding of great relevance to the school practitioner has to do with the low-achieving student's declining need for additional time and help. If, in other words, we provide the potential failure with special assistance early, his need for such assistance will gradually be eliminated. From an economic point of view, therefore, it may be conjectured that compensating activities, in the earliest grades, are the best investment we can make. Such an investment would lead, in time, to "situations in which the crutch of additional time and help is gradually discarded until most of the students learn easily without the need of such learning aids."

Perhaps the classic question of our art is, Why do some students learn and others not? Bloom provides us with an answer by pointing out that entry behaviors (previous cognitive learnings), affective entry characteristics (the learner's previous success or failure), and quality of instruction (the teacher's effectiveness) are the determining factors. Further, his research data indicates that prior cognitive achievement—that is, the student's grasp of prerequisite knowledge—is roughly twice as important as the other two factors. It should be remembered, however, that these percentages relate to the student's cognitive learning; there is another perspective to the data that is equally significant. Bloom discovered, for example, that "unsuccessful experiences in school guarantee that the individual will develop a negative academic self-concept and increase the probabilities that he will have a generally negative self-concept." And, of greater importance, Bloom speculates that continual success or failure in school will have profound effects on the child's personality and mental health: "If the school environment provides the individual with evidence of his adequacy over a number of years and especially in the first six years, there is some evidence that this provides a type of immunization against mental illness for an indefinite period of time." The impact of academic success or failure, consequently, goes far beyond learning the multiplication tables or historical fact.

It is essential, on this point, that we not minimize the close interrelationship between academic success and affect. Bloom notes, illustratively, that "the student typically gains his perceptions about how well he is doing from his position within a group of his peers." What this means, obviously, is that a healthy self-concept—at least in Bloom's lexicon—depends upon previous success in specific areas in relation to others. As a result, artificial situations that attempt to inculcate a feeling of personal worth through "awareness experience" and similar contrivances, will have only limited benefit. It is successful academic learning, in brief, that best generates the affective entry characteristics that lead to further cognitive achievement. The student's feelings about himself, and his belief in his own learning capabilities, come from the external judgments that are communicated by his teachers, parents, and friends. Thus, it may well be that we need to rethink our criteria for bestowing the symbols of failure and success in school. Because a very low grade is likely to have a long-range effect on the student's self-confidence, as well as on his subsequent learning, our basis for labeling and communicating a particular level of student performance as a failure may need to be carefully rethought. The benefits that come from low grades and marks are, at best, questionable.

A word or two also should be said regarding Bloom's evidence on the quality of instruction. In an imaginative departure from conventional research technique, Bloom used an ideal tutor as his model of good teaching. From this model, he deduced that effective teachers make abundant use of cues that clarify the learning task for the student; they provide the learner with many opportunities to practice the responses to be learned; and they use a variety of reinforcements, both positive and negative, as well as both intrinsic and extrinsic. From the point of view of teacher continuing education, accordingly, Bloom's evidence provides rich food for thought. Both preservice and in-service training programs would do well to place a heavy emphasis upon these three sets of pedagogical skills, and the instructional techniques associated with them. Finally—and most important—it would be a tragic oversight if we did not take great pains to familiarize teachers with the influence their valuative judgments have on the lives of their students.

6.

It is not softness and ease that will put an end to the educational alienation of the young, it is a firmer connection with the real world and with the events that to them matter most. We must create a school that has meaning in the child's own context and that allows him to discover himself.

chapter 6
WHAT IS A TAOISTIC TEACHER?
·
Abraham Maslow

EDITOR'S PREFACE

Abraham Maslow's chapter had its seeds in a conference in Palo Alto, California, sponsored by the Center for Coordinated Education, in April 1970. On that occasion, Maslow and I engaged in a dialogue for one of the conference's general sessions. Dialogue is not precisely the word, for in reality I interviewed Maslow, seeking to elicit from his fertile mind some new ideas on the subject at hand.

Shortly after the conference, Abraham Maslow and I talked at length on two other occasions. We taped our discussions for Maslow's use of the transcriptions in preparing his manuscript for this volume. The vagaries of fate what they are, Maslow died a fortnight after our final conversation.

With the transcriptions as a point of departure, this chapter was edited by Dr. Frances

Conn, a gifted and sensitive student of the subject. Maslow, I believe, would have applauded her efforts.

I CALL MYSELF a researcher, but I must qualify the term. I'm a reconnaissance man, a Daniel Boone. I enjoy being the first into the wilderness. The territory I have been scouting lies in a direction different from that occupied by the two theories of human nature that dominate psychology today. The classical theory is behavioristic, and mechanomorphic in the tradition of J.B. Watson, C.L. Hull, and B.F. Skinner. A second philosophy derives from the work of Freud; it is the psychodynamic or depth psychology. What I have to offer to teachers is a point of view, an image of man, a conception of human nature. It is essentially a Taoistic point of view. The term is inaccurate as any of half a dozen others I might have chosen would be, because what I am trying to describe is not a single concept, but a whole syndrome, a set of attitudes.

Essentially, it is the humanistic conception of psychology. It is an existential, phenomenological conception of man. And at the heart of this general point of view toward people is great hope for them, great trust in them. This point of view recognizes all sorts of wonderful possibilities in people, potentialities that in the past were not fulfilled because when people were wonderful it was considered a kind of supernatural accident, not intrinsic to human nature itself.

With this great hope for the potentialities of the person comes a great trust in the wisdom of the body, the wisdom of self-choice. There is trust that man has the tendency to grow, to self-actualize, to seek excellence, to seek virtue, goodness, perfection. And where there is a trust in human beings, there is a willingness to leave them alone. It is this willingness that I identify as the classical Taoistic attitude.

We have an imposing body of data to suggest that we haven't trusted people enough. In many situations ranging from army studies on the self-selection of bomber crews in World War II to J.L. Moreno's work on delinquent girls choosing each other, we find evidence of the wisdom of the body.

I have a grandchild whom I've been watching with great fascination. This child has taken me back to memories of my children as babies thirty years ago. I learned that if I wanted to know what was good for them, I should let them tell me, for instance, when it was time to go to sleep, whether they would eat this or that, whether to play with one game or another. This yielding, let-be attitude is difficult to describe and harder to practice. It's difficult to give up our manipulation, control, intrusion. We know that we attempt to master nature rather than yielding to it or being harmonious with it. We do not always recognize this same approach in dealing with people. It is the let-be attitude that I have called the Taoistic attitude.

The thrust of what we're learning in humanistic psychology is the extent of individual differences within the species. On the one hand is the move toward specieshood, toward the qualities we all have in common. Everybody needs to be loved, every human being. On the other hand there is the move toward self-actualization, to be different from everyone else, to uncover one's own temperamental, constitutional, genetic differences. From Carl Rogers and the New England Transcendentalists both comes this awareness: specieshood discovered at a deep enough level reveals selfhood as well. And the third-force psychology maintains that both searches must be carried on simultaneously. The Taoistic approach permits one to sit with thirty different people and allow them to follow thirty different ways of life.

I'm hopeless with numbers; I've always had trouble with numbers. I can't remember them; I'm not interested in them. It's something constitutional or genetic, from my earliest days. So what? I forgive myself for it. I learned the minimum I had to. I did not become a mathematician; I'm a poor statistician. But I'm good at something else, and I've built on my own capabilities rather than trying to overcome defects.

This is implied in the Taoistic approach—not only accepting the style of another person, but accepting the style of nature, the style of things as they are. If you trust them sufficiently—that includes birds, trees, monkeys, human beings—then you discover there is considerable wisdom of the body, self-reparation and self-healing. It requires that kind of Taoistic trust to keep from interfering. With that kind of trust, inevitably you move toward each person as an individual. Taoism means respect for yourself as well, paying attention to your own impulses. If you can't do something, forgive the defect and build on your strength. If something is forced on you, resist. A tree wants to grow up, not sideways, and so it pushes up. That is its way. And if you want to be helpful, you get out of its way.

The humanistic psychologist conceives of the human being as having an essence, a real self to be discovered and actualized. This self must be sought for and uncovered. This view totally rejects the behaviorists' *tabula rasa* notions that assume a human being to be a passive clay to be shaped, controlled, modified by external agents. It rejects, too, the Freudian conception of instincts, positing instead the conception of basic needs that must be gratified if the person is to become fully human and to grow well. The teacher, then, would be one who helps a person discover what is already in him, not a shaper of persons into prearranged forms in accordance with *a priori* notions.

Generated by this new humanistic philosophy is also a new conception of learning, of teaching, and of education. Stated simply, such a concept holds that the function of education, the goal of education—the human goal, the humanistic goal, the goal so far as human beings are concerned—is ultimately the self-actualization of a person, the becoming fully human, the development of the fullest height that the human species can stand up to or that the particular individual can come to. In a less technical way, it is helping the person to become the best that he is able to become.

This is not easy. Teachers and other kinds of professionals suffer from having been indoctrinated into a mastering, manipulating, controlling outlook toward nature, toward people, especially toward children. Helping is actually a very, very difficult thing to do. Frequently, the best thing to do by way of helping other people is keep your hands off. Stay out of the way. Helping, truly helping in the Taoistic fashion, is an art. And one thing is clear—I can report this empirically—the best helpers of other people are the most highly evolved, healthiest, strongest, most fully developed people. Therefore, if you want to help others whether as teacher, or psychologist, or parent, or doctor, if you're in the helping professions, which every human being should be as amateur or professional, clearly one part of your job is to become a better person. The better person you are, the less neurotic you are, the less need you have to manipulate, control, and force people into limitations of yourself rather than help them grow in their own style.

The other aspect of the situation is that in order to help yourself become a better person, in order to develop personal growth, you must help other people. This is the yin and the yang, the simultaneous growing of oneself by helping others to grow. And the healthier a person grows, the more he enjoys helping others to grow. It is reflexive. The Taoistic attitude is a modest one, recognizing, even as one helps others, that ultimately they are autonomous agents and must help themselves and that the best way to help them is to be available for them, letting them discover what they themselves are like, what they themselves want to do, what are their talents, and tastes, and judgments, and capacities.

There are two great legends in Buddhism. In one, Buddha sat under the tree and had his great mystic experiences, his great illuminations. He saw the truth, was forever enlightened, and, so to speak, ascended and entered into heaven. Nirvana.

The other legend, which I prefer, is the Bodhisattvic legend. In this Buddha sat under the tree, saw the truth, ascended to heaven, and at the gates of heaven, out of compassion for mankind, renounced heaven and came back to help. The Bodhisattvic path, then, is the path of the helper, the right helper.

Part of the teacher's motivation to help his students may well grow from his own deficiency needs— for safety, for security, for affection, for belonging, for liking, for loving. Basic needs are part of our essence, our human nature. If we learn to accept that we have these needs—in the same sense that we have five fingers instead of six, as a fact of life—then I see no danger. The recognition that we need constant narcissistic supplies, as the psychoanalysts call them, can be the basis for a kind of modesty about ourselves, a humility. We can recognize that we are fallible human beings. Consciousness protects us against the destructive and pathogenic character of our repressions. If we don't have to repress the fact that we enjoy affection, then there is no danger. That, of course, is the great Freudian lesson.

I think we can teach this, bring deficiency needs to the same level of recognition as the fact that we need so much Vitamin B or calcium. The problem arises when there are defenses against recognizing our own natures. The person who feels that he has to put on a surface of toughness, strongness, self-sufficiency, who must project the image of needing no one, of never being hurt, is a source of danger to himself and to those with whom he comes in contact.

I am more concerned with the tendency for people to repress their highest motivations. We are ashamed to be corny, to be sentimental, to feel kind, altruistic, generous, affectionate. This seems especially true in our culture and for our young people. These youngsters, the nicest ones, the healthiest ones, are torn and they experience great conflict because they are essentially—dare I use the word in 1970?—virtuous. They're good kids; they're kind; they tend not to hate. They are very uneasy with the more general meanness that is apt to show itself in late adolescence. The herd quality and the gang quality repel them, but they are caught in between, not daring to show openly their generosity or affection or altruism.

Ours is essentially a good society, certainly the best large society in the history of mankind. And yet we run ourselves down. In Congress it is not advisable to suggest we might help other nations unless we can demonstrate that it is in our own interest. "It's in the national interest," congressmen will say, and they will not dare to say that it is in the international interest. Yet they feel that to be the case. They, too, have donned the chameleon coat of toughness and materialism. Here again, insight is the answer, an awareness of our metamotivations, of our virtuous feelings.

The history of increasing bureaucratization and technology in teaching has led to a hierarchical and authoritarian organization in the schools. In such a climate it is difficult for teachers to acknowledge their metamotivations. Increasingly teaching is described in terms of contracts and job specifications. But in industry the humanistic approach is beginning to be felt. More and more supervisors and bosses are being cut out and decisions are moving to the point where the production is being done. As Taoistic trust develops in the educational enterprise, there would be more leeway given to teachers, less regard for centralization, fewer orders coming from a rule book. Of course there will be problems, and the Taoistic approach has never been tried well enough so that we can tell what proportion of the population could function well under those circumstances and what proportion would collapse.

In establishing the psychology department and a graduate program in psychology in a new university, free of tradition and preconception, I had an opportunity to experiment with a Taoistic approach to teaching. I worked with the graduate program for about ten years, and I have some data to show those for whom such a program works and those for whom it does not.

We began with a purely Taoistic approach, in the Summerhill tradition. It offered close to total freedom to people who said they were committed to psychology. The assumption was that they loved psychology, wanted to be psychologists, and what would be best for them would be the freedom to choose their own way. The faculty was there in the role of consultants, and students were invited to use us, squeeze the juice from us.

This approach worked beautifully for approximately one-third of our graduate students. It was an unleashing. These students produced doctoral dissertations that were truly contributions to knowledge, ground-breaking dissertations.

For 25 percent of our students the program was a total failure. But I learned from this the kinds of persons with whom it did not work, the kinds of persons for whom the Taoistic approach would not work. It did not work for overly passive people. Passive people collapse under freedom.

It didn't work for authoritarian personalities either. They could not believe that it was our pleasure to see them grow. They continually sought out people and begged to be told what to do. It didn't work for psychopaths. The psychopathic personality, in its milder version, regards the giving of freedom as a sign of weakness, of foolishness. Out of this sense, the mildly psychopathic would seek to sabotage the program for fun. Finally, it fails with paranoids who cannot bear freedom.

From this experience, slowly and with great difficulty, I learned to make the modifications that I have called American Taoism. With this modification, one stays as nonintrusive as possible, as person-respecting as possible, yet takes into account the existence of psychopathology. Even in a Taoistic atmosphere, human sickness and human evil, human folly, greed, and laziness exist. And because they exist, they must be handled. The formula for American

Taoism is to permit freedom within varying degrees of very firm limits.

One serious problem in education is that we have inherited from various sources a kind of mistrust of force, power, decisiveness, strength. We tend to regard them as somehow intrinsically evil. They are not.

There is no inconsistency in this view. One can enjoy the self-actualization of others, take pleasure in watching people grow in their own pattern, their own style. It is even possible, while wondering what kind of person will develop, to love that new person in advance, as a child to be can be loved even before it is conceived. What will it be? Will it be a dancer, or chemist, or automotive technician? And it's possible with the Taoistic attitude to be perfectly willing to help it to be whatever nature, and genes, and environment are going to make it be. There is Taoistic pleasure in watching simultaneously the development of an oak tree, a rosebush, and a daffodil with the recognition that it would be stupid and futile to interfere and try to make the rosebush turn into an oak. This attitude is completely compatible with, and requires as a necessary supplement, a carefully integrated notion of authority and power. It requires an awareness of human evil and human pathology. There is a necessary use of force. I feel no discomfort in talking in one sentence about Taoism and in the next about discipline; it is easy to make a pattern of the two of them.

Imagine that you have children in a dangerous environment. Picture a large playpen that keeps the children off the street, out of danger from falling into wells or swimming pools. But within that playpen there is total freedom. In this sense, the freedom can be total and the limits absolute, and there would be no contradiction. In the same way there is no contradiction between Taoism and discipline.

To understand the breadth of the role of the teacher, a differentiation has to be made between extrinsic learning and intrinsic learning. The former is content education, skill education. It is the learning described in chapters on learning theory. It is controlled from the outside, a learning of impersonal associations, and it is extrinsic to the personality of the learner. In this learning it is the teacher who is active, shaping the learner. Extrinsic learning is based on the goals of the teacher, not on the values of the learner.

Intrinsic learning, on the other hand, is learning to be and to become a human being, and a particular human being. It is the learning that accompanies the profound personal experiences in our lives. These learnings are unique instances, not the results of drill and repetitions. In my own life I think of the death of my father, the birth of my children, and of my grandchild, as such moments. In such experiences do we discover who we are, what we are, what we might become.

As I go back over my own life, I find that my greatest educational experiences, the ones I value most in retrospect, were highly personal, highly subjective, very poignant combinations of the emotional and the cognitive. Some great insight was accompanied by all sorts of autonomic nervous system fireworks that felt very good at the time and which left as a residue the insight that has remained with me forever. This is what I call an intrinsic learning experience.

It would be ideal to combine the two learnings and integrate them, so that personal growth can take place through content and skill education and simultaneously with it. It would be possible, though difficult, to teach many subjects—history, biology, astronomy, for example—so as to stress personal discovery, the joy of insight, personal growth, and illumination. Surely this is one of the pressing tasks for educators. To facilitate that task, however, it seems well to stress the different educational goals of the person seeking growth to self-actualization, full humanness, toward identity, toward a personal system of values on the one hand and, on the other, the presumably mature person who, having achieved his identity, has committed himself to his "way." The former seeks to learn what to do with his life; the latter has already made this decision and seeks to actualize his self through becoming, for example, a good physician, rather than a poor one, a good mechanic rather than a bumbler.

For me, the sudden falling in love with psychology came in one moment. Thereafter, I was willing to submit myself to discipline, take courses I did not like, study with professors some of whom were paranoid. I was willing to do this because I could learn from them. Before my commitment to psychology as my life's work, I was looking for teachers who were sympathetic, who would listen to an adolescent, who were warm and fatherly. Once I knew, discovered intrinsically, that psychology was to be my profession, I wanted all the knowledge and skill I could acquire.

It would appear that personal growth should be the focus of early education—in kindergarten and the first grades. Nurturing in children the tendency to express, to improvise, to be aware of sensory stimulation should be done early. Much of the Esalen experience, it seems to me, is reparative work for adults who did not have these early growth opportunities.

I share with other scholars an uneasiness over some misuses of this Esalen-type education. In the wrong hands it can lead to antiintellectualism, antiwork. Spontaneity (the impulses from our best self) gets confused with impulsivity and acting out (the impulses from our sick self) and there is then no way to tell the difference.

Impatience, especially the built-in impatience of youth, dictates shortcuts of all kinds. The sudden insight becomes "all" and the patient and disciplined "working through" is postponed or devalued. Instead of being "surprised by joy," "turning on" is scheduled, promised, advertised, sold, hustled into being, and can get to be regarded as a commodity.

Much of what is called personal growth education is essentially experimental, an attempt to discover more about human nature. There are those, however, who assume we know more than we do and apply the techniques unquestioningly. There is a trend among some, for example, to consider competence and training as irrelevant or unnecessary. Young people particularly are eager to take shortcuts to spontaneity, overlooking the fact that its chief proponents, Carl Rogers or Aldous Huxley, for example, see spontaneity as a consequence of disciplined, hard work. The growing insistence of students that they be stimulated, inspired, entertained by the teacher may be taken as a symptom of the extreme child-centering of recent decades. The great task of education is so to humanize content education that its relevance is felt.

The classical curriculum can be approached with children in a way that will "turn them on" as the great ones in each field were illumined. An astronomer thrills and shivers with his experience in astronomy. My course in music in college opened me up to music, and I think this can be done even with arithmetic for children. Certainly higher mathematics can be taught in almost a religious way. In the highest values of Spinoza you think of mathematics as the study of pure elegance, pure beauty, harmony, not as rote learning of instruments, means, techniques.

Music education is the best example. For many people, music is a source of peak experiences, of autonomic reactions. In music education we must avoid desacralizing and demythologizing music. Music education can be teaching for pleasure, for happiness, for ecstasy. And the teaching of music in this manner can be a model for all the curriculum.

Paleontology can be just as beautiful, just as peak-producing as music. So can history, or anthropology (in the sense of learning another culture), social anthropology, or the study of science. The creative scientist lives by peak experiences. He lives for the moments of glory when a problem solves itself, when suddenly through a microscope he sees things in a very different way, the moments of revelation, of illumination, insight, understanding, ecstasy. These are vital for him. Scientists are very, very shy and embarrassed about this. They refuse to talk about this in public. It takes a delicate kind of midwifery to get these things out, but I have gotten them out. They are there, and if one can manage to convince a creative scientist that he is not going to be laughed at for these things, then he will blushingly admit he is having a high emotional experience.

Effective education in music, art, dancing, and rhythm is intrinsically closer than the usual "core curriculum" to intrinsic education of the kind that I am talking about, of learning one's identity as an essential part of education. If education doesn't do that, it is useless. Education is learning to grow, learning what to grow toward, learning what is good and bad, learning what is desirable and undesirable, learning what to choose and what not to choose. In this realm of intrinsic learning, intrinsic teaching, and intrinsic education I think that the arts, and especially the ones that I have mentioned, are so close to our psychological and biological core, so close to this identity, this biological identity, that rather than think of these courses as a sort of whipped cream or luxury, they must become basic experiences in education. I mean that this kind of education can be a glimpse into the infinite, into ultimate values.

If teachers are going to be able to open their pupils to peak experiences, they must first learn to recognize them and to nurture them in their own lives. New data have been gathered and we now know that it is not necessary to be in the pantheon of self-actualization to have peak experiences. In natural childbirth, for instance, women who are not necessarily highly evolved were able to achieve the ecstasy of the experience. What is necessary is neither to fear the experience nor to regard it as an attack of indigestion or schizophrenia. If we open ourselves to them, peak experiences at various levels and intensities are difficult to avoid.

When I have lectured to groups about the phenomenon in a very positive way and approving manner, people begin to remember having had peak experiences. They recall instances to which they have never given that label. It is as if a reassuring father had said, "It's all right to have these experiences," and suddenly they start coming to mind. This is not unlike someone in psychoanalysis beginning to remember dreams that previously he had not.

We do have empirical evidence about peak experiences. It is derived from questions put to various general populations. One of our investigators asked, "Have you experienced transcendent ecstasy?" Contrary to what might be expected as response—silence, embarrassment, and so forth—there were many affirmative answers. These transcendent ecstasies had all been kept private because there was no acceptable way of talking about them in public.

Investigation has revealed a variety of triggers for peak experiences. Indeed, the list is so large that one must generalize. It appears that any experience of excellence, perfection, of moving toward perfect values tends to produce a peak experience. One male subject reported a feeling of ecstasy when in a football game he pulled free from the line and ran into the open. Women describe having babies at the breast in the same kind of poetic terms.

While we do not have systematic data on peak experiences in children, there is sufficient anecdotal evidence to allow us to be confident that children do have such experiences. It may well be that they have them more frequently than adults. In the early years they derive largely from sensory stimulation: color, rhythm, sound. The words *wonder, awe, absorption, fascination* come to mind to characterize these experiences as intrinsic rewards, moments when both cognitive and personal growth take place. The humanistic educator, the Taoistic teacher, would welcome the fascination of children, their jags and enthusiasms. And from the interest of their teachers, the children would learn to value the moments of illumination, the peak moments that can give impetus to and meaning for the more routine demands of the classical curriculum.

It is clear that only some teachers would be able to carry out a Taoistic approach. Some would make it into something hierarchical and bureaucratic. The obsessionals would continue to go by the book. There are, after all, obsessionals in the world. And so I would suppose that a large school system would have to be pluralistic in approach, and experimental. In any group of teachers there will be some who will be comfortable with a Summerhill-type approach and some who will not.

Many teachers already in the field have developed habits and traditions that are incompatible with the let-be philosophy of Taoism. There is little doubt that the average American citizen is too up tight about too many things, but there can be reparative work. For instance, there could be built into in-service training encounter groups, psychodrama groups.

There are some difficult decisions to make. We're dealing with a kind of battlefield surgery. There is so much money, so much time for therapeutic work, so much time for T-groups. The experience with industry is that the humanistic, humane, essentially democratic, and Taoistic way of life is entering, but very slowly. Perhaps 5 percent of industry is affected, and 95 percent is resisting. I suspect that the pattern may be similar in the schools. In the interim, I see no reason for not having within conventional school systems the experimental school. With a pluralistic and experimental attitude, there is no reason why we could not establish pilot schools. Let teachers who wish to experiment do so. The others can continue in traditional ways. Have one demonstration school and then watch it. Have good assessment and good evaluation.

At this point we simply don't know enough about many of the innovations: team teaching, inductive inquiry, individualized instruction, and the like. We don't know enough about which is better for whom, when, where, and why. Because this is the case, I should think a principal might suggest an innovation rather than force one on a school staff. He could ask who would like to try a new approach, and let that person volunteer. Or if the situation made it necessary for everyone to be involved with a new approach, he would be modest about presenting it, recommending a truly experimental attitude. This would be a realistic, truthful, honest attitude with no fakery, no hard sell. When we have some experimental evidence about how individual innovations work, then we can say with some confidence, "This works for nine out of ten people, let's try it." The more we know, the stronger can be our urging of others to try it. This would be part of the same Taoistic regime. Try it out. If it does not work for you, then you need not use it.

We need to look at educational innovations now as opportunities to learn. We can learn from the Santa Cruz experiment. Let the students run it as a town meeting, by acclamation. Let us see how it works.

I learned a great deal from the Roachdale experiment in Toronto. The community was run in a hippie style: no force, no money. Force is evil, money is evil. You must give anybody anything he asks for. They attracted every hoodlum within a two hundred-mile radius. What happened? The place fell apart. This same thing happened in Haight-Ashbury. These experiments are valuable if we learn from them, write it down, and pass it on.

We have a large body of plausible theory and not enough fact. We have had enough experience to say that the Taoistic way appears a better way, but not enough confidence to force it on other people even if force were compatible with Taoism.

I must stress again that I am a theorist. What I have presented are points of view based on plausibility derived from a certain amount of data. What is essential is the feedback. How does it work? We need collaboration between humanistic psychology and education. The teacher, the practitioner, is the Supreme Court, the tester, the one who ultimately decides whether this is wisdom or nonsense. It is the teacher who can confirm or disconfirm the theory. The person who writes freely and lectures is giving forth. He needs feedback from the practitioners in the field. Only such feedback, only a dialogue between the theorist and the educator, can assure sufficient empirical grounding.

editor's comments

THERE IS A SPECIAL poignancy to this piece of prose because it may very well be Abraham Maslow's last writing. Should this be the case, it is a happy choice—it is, in the purest sense, what I think of as vintage Maslow. We have here, in elegant form, the essence of the humanistic philosophy—there is "a real self to be discovered and actualized." This, for Maslow, was what education is all about. The child is to be regarded not as clay to be shaped, but as a living organism that must, in its own way, become fully human.

Maslow was deeply concerned about what he regarded as a misconception of the teacher's purpose. He was worried about teacher training that converted the teacher into a controlling manipulator. Having devoted a lifetime to his own helping profession, and viewing teaching as a similar endeavor, he had concluded that "helping" was an exceedingly difficult and delicate art. The master stroke of craftsmanship, he believed, lay in knowing when to intervene and when to "keep hands off."

From this idea, we can derive implications for both curriculum and teacher training. With regard to the curriculum, schooling must provide the learner with abundant opportunities to find himself, allowing limitless chances to survive failure until, sooner or later, success materializes. Unrestricted time and opportunity to actualize, thought Maslow, was a modest price to pay for ultimate success. And with respect to the second clue, enormous attention must be given in the preparation of teachers to that facet of teaching finesse that involves knowing when—and how —to superimpose teacher control on the child's own self-control. The critical danger is that the teacher's own personal needs—rather than the child's—will prevail. It is for this reason that Maslow felt that "the best helpers of other people are the most highly evolved, healthiest, strongest, most fully developed people."

Maslow had a deep and abiding faith in man's inherent goodness; but he was neither naive nor soft minded. He went to a considerable effort, for example, to make it clear that trust in man's fundamental goodness did not imply mistrust of force, power, or strength. His passion for hard work, both in himself and his students, was legendary. Not unmindful of human folly and evil, Maslow was totally opposed to unlicensed freedom. He had learned, in short, that freedom was a mixed blessing; for some, it fertilized a remarkable flowering, but for others, it provoked self-defeat. The passive, the authoritarian, the psychopath, the paranoid—all these do badly with an excess of freedom. He was moved, therefore, to urge that freedom be permitted within varying degrees of limits: "One stays as nonintrusive as possible, as person-respecting as possible, yet takes into account the existence of psychopathology." One cannot help but suspect that the American teacher, who probably came to much the same conclusion through experience, will applaud Maslow's reservations about the uses and abuses of children's autonomy and freedom.

Our society has a questionable fondness for diatribe, for debate, and for controversy. We seem to take special delight in creating opposing camps and in nurturing competitiveness between them. It is as if we viewed scholarly inquiry as a jousting match in which one side must defeat the other. Maslow remarked one day, somewhat wistfully, that "Skinner and I are really quite similar in our outlooks—it is our graduate students who are so far apart." As such, he saw much to be admired in the theories of, not only Skinner, but of Carl Rogers, Jerome Bruner, Jean Piaget, and Robert Gagne. It would be a great error, consequently, to view Maslow's conception of humanistic psychology as antithetical to rigorous scholarship and cognition. He preferred, in his own lexicon, to regard facts and feelings as "intrinsic and extrinsic learning." He believed that neither should dominate the other. Extrinsic learning—that based upon the curricular objectives of the teacher—is essential to a well-informed mind. Intrinsic learning—that based upon the pivotal experiences through which we come to know ourselves—is equally indispensable to becoming fully human. He thought it eminently possible—albeit difficult—that both kinds of learning might go on at the same time. More than anything else, he felt, a school ought to help the individual to find himself; to begin and continue the task of becoming—to actualize. In this sense, he would have been equally dismayed with the happy incompetent and the unhappy expert.

"The great task of education is so to humanize content education that its relevance is felt." It is in this sentence that the spirit of Maslow's expectations of schooling show most clearly. Relevance is to be attained not by coating substantive ideas with sugar, not by transforming the classroom into an entertainment center, nor by the thoughtless worship of spontaneity, but by searching— long and hard—for the natural seductiveness of the subject matter itself.

It is revealing, I think, that Maslow sees fit near the end of his chapter to observe that the school he describes will not be suitable for either all students or all teachers. Too wise to assume that education could negate the variations of personality, Maslow was ready to grant those who find comfort in structure their own way.

He further sensed that an authentic humanistic school might be just the other side of the Utopian border, and favored, therefore, an experimental school—within the conventional system—that might explore the yet unbroken ground. Such a school, he felt, might become a place in which to evolve new curricula, new techniques, and—of greatest importance—diagnostic criteria for determining what sorts of students and teachers would thrive in such an atmosphere. Convinced that both a pluralistic school system and the individualization of instruction within these differing schools were desirable, he foresaw that neither could be achieved without a workable method of ensuring a good "fit" of teacher, curriculum, and child. Maslow recognized that our resources of time, energy, and money were limited, and thus natural selection might be too inefficient and cumbersome. There is an inescapable need for experimentation, for scientific study, and for hard, verifiable fact: visionary ideas and good intentions are not enough.

Abraham Maslow contributed uniquely to our understanding of the human potential. It would be tragic indeed if we reduced his ideas to mere platitudes, or if we overlooked the need to support, reinforce, and modify them through, as he called it, "sufficient empirical grounding."

7.

Men act on the basis of what they think and feel. The present school, dedicated to responsible and intelligent action, concerns itself chiefly with what children think. But their feelings—now chiefly ignored—exert a profound influence on their behavior. It is imperative, therefore, that as we reform the school we strike a healthier balance between affect and cognition.

chapter 7
INVOLVING FANTASIES AND FEELINGS
.
Richard M. Jones

WHEN I BEGAN writing *Fantasy and Feeling in Education*[1] in 1965, part of the motivation stemmed from noting how remarkably seldom these important parts of the learning process were engaged in American schoolrooms or acknowledged in curriculum planning projects. However, it soon became clear that systematic efforts to involve these more personal sides of children's interests in their formal schooling were soon to become more numerous and less controversial. Terry Borton, Eli Bower, George Isaac Brown, Barbara Ellis Long, Sheldon Roen, Robert Samples, and others in the humanistic psychology movement were starting to be listened to and followed. Their variety notwithstanding, all of these efforts can, I think, be traced to the widespread influence of psychotherapy and allied techniques in

---

1. Richard M. Jones, *Fantasy and Feeling in Education* (New York: Harper and Row, 1968); and Richard M. Jones, ed., *Contemporary Educational Psychology* (New York: Harper and Row, 1966).

American culture generally, and the resulting application of psychotherapeutic concepts and methods to
educational practices in particular.

The first sign that knowledge gained from psychotherapy might be suggestive of educational reforms
was Freud's observation of an affinity between the
neurotic process and the creative process. Both were
seen to have their genesis in unconscious conflict.
However, in the one the unconscious conflict was re-
pressed and in the other it was deployed in a distinctive way, described by Freud as follows:

> Co-operation between a preconscious and an
> unconscious impulse, even when the latter is sub-
> ject to very strong repression, may be es-
> tablished if the situation permits of the uncon-
> scious impulse operating in harmony with one of
> the controlling tendencies. The repression is re-
> moved for the occasion, the repressed activity
> being admitted as a reinforcement of the one in-
> tended by the ego. In respect of this single con-
> stellation the unconscious becomes egosyntonic,
> falls in line with the ego, without any change
> taking place in the repression otherwise. The ef-
> fect of the Ucs in this co-operation is unmistaka-
> ble; the reinforced tendencies reveal themselves
> as, in spite of all, different from the normal—
> they make possible achievements of special per-
> fection, and they manifest a resistance in the
> face of opposition similar to that of obsessional
> symptoms.[2]

Ernst Kris was later to describe this process as
"regression in the service of the ego."[3]

2. Sigmund Freud, "The Unconscious," *Collected Papers,* vol. 4
    (London: Hogarth Press, 1949), p. 127.
3. Ernst Kris, "On Preconscious Mental Processes," *Psycho-
    analytic Quarterly* 19 (1950).

It remained for Lawrence Kubie to further systematize this position and to draw its implications for pedagogical reforms. Kubie first drew a set of essential distinctions between conscious, unconscious, and preconscious symbolic processes. Conscious symbolic processes are predominantly verbal, thrive on repetition, and serve primarily the communication of ideas. Unconscious symbolic processes are predominantly nonverbal, also thrive on repetition, and serve primarily to prevent communication by disrupting connections between conscious symbols and their referents. Preconscious symbolic processes are predominantly analogical and therefore serve primarily to diversify the relations between conscious symbols and their referents.

Distinctive of preconscious functions are "their automatic and subtle recordings of multiple perceptions, their automatic recall, their multiple analogic and overlapping linkages, and their direct connections to the autonomic processes which underlie affective states."[4] Kubie conceives preconscious functions to be constantly operative behind the scenes of consciousness and likely to emerge on stage "in states of abstraction, in sleep, in dreams, and as we write, paint, or allow our thoughts to flow in the nonselected paths of free association."[5] Their emergence, however, is conditional:

> Where conscious processes predominate at one end of the spectrum, rigidity is imposed by the fact that conscious symbolic functions are anchored by their precise and literal relationships to specific conceptual and perceptual

4. Lawrence Kubie, *Neurotic Distortion of the Creative Process* (Lawrence, Kans.: University of Kansas Press, 1958), pp. 44-45.
5. Ibid., p. 45.

units. Where unconscious processes predominate at the other end of the spectrum, there is an even more rigid anchorage, but in this instance to unreality. . . . Yet flexibility of symbolic imagery is essential if the symbolic process is to have that creative potential which is our supreme human trait . . . this creative flexibility is made possible predominantly if not exclusively by the free, continuous, and concurrent action of preconscious processes.[6]

The dual imperative for educators who were interested in facilitating creative thought and behavior in school children was then extracted by Kubie:

(1) They must cease their excessive reliance on "drill and grill" routines, which serve to overstrengthen the constraining influences of conscious processes.

(2) They must lift the "conspiracy of silence" to which much of children's emotional lives are subjected throughout school life.

While Kubie found appreciative ears among many educators, few were able to follow his clinical prescriptions to their educational counterparts. The reasons, I think, were: (1) The path that Kubie charted between psychotherapy and education was one-way, and the smell of medicine hovered disconcertingly over it. This was not an atmosphere in which many teachers could be expected to find their own ways. (2) The theory of healthy emotional development, upon which Kubie based his educational imperatives, was largely a product of interpolation between the lines of the psychoanalytic theory of unhealthy emotional development—with all of the connotations of preschool predetermination that this theory carries, and which

6. Ibid., p. 38.

teachers have found so forbidding, because it seems to leave so little room for optimism about what schoolteaching can expect to accomplish.

What is needed then is (1) a perspective that shows the way for mutual commerce between psychotherapy and education, and (2) a theory of healthy human development that can stand on its own good feet.

The first of these I tried to provide in chapter 4 of *Fantasy and Feeling*, entitled "Insight and Outsight." The second I tried to provide in chapter 6, entitled "The Course of Emotional Growth," wherein I relied heavily on the work of Erik Erikson. Judging from the responses of many teachers, both of these attempts seem to have been reasonably successful. Unfortunately, the same cannot be said about the book's final chapter. There I meant to draw from the theoretical formulations and classroom examples of the previous eight chapters a set of clearly stated principles for use by teachers in suggesting and evaluating innovations aimed at involving children's fantasies and feelings in their schooling. But, it seems in retrospect, so intoxicated had I become in quarreling with Jerome Bruner at that point that instead of writing the chapter I had intended I wrote another critique of Bruner. This is known as taking your eye off the ball. It pains me to recognize this; on the other hand it affords an opportunity to say something now that I hope the readers of this volume will find meaningful, and that, in any event, I want very much to say.

PRINCIPLE 1

Instructed involvement in schoolwork of children's fantasies and feelings should be perceived by the teacher and by the children as a means to better learning, and not as an end in itself. Whatever conditions a teacher may improvise to make classroom expression of emotion and private imagery appropriate should also make it relevant to understanding some culturally valued subject matter, or to the mastery of some personally valuable learning skill. Not that there is anything sacred about any particular subject matter nor about any particular learning skill. Only that to encourage subjectivity to the exclusion of objectivity is as discouraging to optimal learning as to encourage objectivity to the exclusion of subjectivity. The latter, as we know all too well, leads to boredom, apathy, or the tacit attitudes of expected failure that John Holt has so movingly described.[7] The former leads to a blurring of the crucial distinctions between anxieties that threaten learning and anxieties that require learning, between routines that stunt and those that comfort, between fantasies that lean toward escapist fictions and fantasies that beckon interesting facts.

PRINCIPLE 2

Particularly effective as stimulants to the natural involvement of children's fantasies and feelings are intellectually honest and significant lessons and materials in the humanities, the arts, and the biological and social sciences. This for the reason that the referents to which the symbols of these areas of knowledge pertain are inherently subjective with respect to the child's ego. In these areas, in other words, if they are clearly represented, there is no need to enlist the child's emotions and fantasies by devious appeals to self-interests. The appeal of these realms of public

7. John Holt, *How Children Fail* (New York: Pitman, 1964).

knowledge to the child's private interests is direct and unavoidable.

PRINCIPLE 3

If a problem, an exercise, or a piece of curricular material could not cause some degree of initial emotional discomfort in some children, it is not likely to stimulate the self-interests of many children. Conversely, if a problem or exercise or piece of curricular material is likely to stimulate the self-interests of many children, it is also likely to cause some degree of initial emotional discomfort in some children. I put the issue this way in order to oppose what can only be called the unconscious avoidance reflex of many teachers in reaction to signs of emotional discomfort in students. Thus, many a promising possibility of enlivening a lesson by way of focusing on its emotionally provocative aspects is aborted, because of the teacher's determination "not to threaten the children." Let us be very clear on what it is that threatens children. A feeling or image that cannot be controlled is frightening; a feeling or image that cannot be shared is estranging; a feeling or image that cannot be put to work is, in a school setting, belittling. These conditions do threaten children. But do not blame these conditions, when they exist, on curricula. Blame them, instead, on the teacher who lets it be feared that anything under her guidance could get out of control; or who has failed to create an atmosphere in which the children may choose to share their feelings and private thoughts, free of the illusion that this must lead to acting them out; or, worse, whose command of her subject matter is so shallow as to be unable to see the relevance to it of all possible human feelings and images.

PRINCIPLE 4

Conversely, creating conditions that both encour-age and instruct children in the control, sharing, and use of their emotions and images in relation to their schooling is the surest way of addressing education to the "whole child." What I wish to emphasize here is that the general formula could not be followed by a teacher, much less could original applications of the formula be expected to occur to a teacher, who did not first perceive signs of emotional discomfort in children as opportunities to be cultivated rather than as dangers to be avoided. After all, such signs are precisely indicative of the "schematic disequilibrium" that Piaget has shown to be the first necessary phase of human adaption to novelty. Not to invite such mental states at all is to altogether forfeit one's teaching responsibilities; to invite them and then avoid them is, at worst, to lock the child into a defen-sive posture in respect to this or that item of knowl-edge. At best, it is to leave the child to his chances of finding some untutored way from a helpless or es-tranged response to some new aspect of his world toward mastery and shared enjoyment.

PRINCIPLE 5

A teacher's lesson plans should regularly include exercises that encourage and reward interesting as well as "right" responses. This is no more than to un-derscore what has long been obvious to students of "creativity." Namely, that creative thinking involves divergent as well as convergent thinking; digression as well as concentration; negation as well as affirma-tion; the formation of concepts as well as the attain-ment of concepts—in short, invention as well as dis-covery. The difficulty experienced by teachers in respect to this manifold principle has not been one of credibility but one of application. Most teachers who have read or heard of the researches of J.W. Getzels and Philip W. Jackson, Frank Barron, Edith Weiskopf-Joelson, Calvin Taylor, and Abraham Maslow, among many others, find the validity of their rhetoric self-evident. But there has been a curious lack of classroom improvisations by teachers themselves showing the way from persuasive rhetoric to effective methods. Curious, because the general strategy is so clearly indicated and so simple: the inclusion in routine recitation, discussion, assignment, and evaluation procedures of the use of metaphor, analogy, paraphrase, and other thought processes the function of which is to make the strange familiar and the familiar strange; and occasional attention to the involuntary generic forms of these thought processes—the dream, the reverie, the image. Children should be led to expect that when asked to say what a thing is, it is not only permissible but frequently desirable to say what it *is like,* what it is *as if,* what it is not but could more enjoyably be thought as, what it reminds one of or makes one feel; what, in short, it is *as it were.* Despite everything most children usually learn to say what enough things "are," to get from grade to grade and to show acceptable progress on "achievement" tests, whether they understand what these things mean or not. But the current "relevance crisis" in American higher education tells us with unmistakable clarity that most children are not learning how to take much interest in what things are, are not learning how to turn the realities of their culture into personally valued meanings. And as some recent experimental programs in college education have painfully discovered, it is impossible to teach young adults the meaning of things. Young adults can only be helped to find their own meanings. And more often than not, by young adulthood it is too late, if there has been no earlier practice in the fundamentals of the art. Therefore, once a teacher has incorporated regular appeals to the "as if" in her classroom, she is well advised to lavish even more attention on interesting digressions to and from correct answers than on the answers themselves. However, as simple and well documented as is this advice, I bring little optimism to hopes of its widespread acceptance so deep-seated seems to be American education's addiction to correct answers.

PRINCIPLE 6

Several advantages accrue to these exercises being routine rather than exceptional: (1) The children come to associate their fantasy life with their work life. This association is more than mentally healthy. (2) The onus of permissiveness is removed, and replaced by the more credible influence of authority. (Children know that we permit them what may or may not be good for them, but when there is no questioning the goodness of something, we simply set aside time for it.) (3) The children can pace themselves; momentarily useful defenses, sometimes cloaked by otherwise fetching metaphors, need not harden for lack of the right moment to drop them. (4) The teacher can directly coordinate the products of such exercises to immediately relevant learning tasks. In short, much of the guesswork is removed from the teacher's task of cultivating individual discovery.

PRINCIPLE 7

Symbolization is not synonymous with verbalization. Words may be our most advanced symbols, but we know how empty they can become when cut off from their nonverbal roots, i.e., from what Bruner has termed their enactive and iconic referents. In seeking to devise ways to invite divergent thought processes more regularly into classroom procedures, therefore, the teacher should aspire to the entertainment of more than figures of speech. Drawing, painting, modeling, music, dance, drama, pantomime, and other forms of nonverbal symbolization should all find their place. I am aware that in many schools a portion of the children's time is spent in art, dance, drama, and music classes. I am also aware, however, that these activities are most often intended to serve cathartic functions only, and are likely, therefore, to remain set off in the minds of children from their heavier academic duties. All too often, in fact, such classes are led by visiting specialists with whom the teacher of first authority shares little, if any, professional liaison. What I have in mind is something a little closer to the curricular vest, and conducted by the teacher of first authority, whether in conjunction with art, drama, dance, and music classes, or not. In this way the chances will be increased that all three of Piaget's systems for processing information and representing knowledge—the sensori-motor, the concrete-operational, and the formal-operational—will get in on the educational act.

PRINCIPLE 8

Applications of these principles for increasing the involvement of children's self-interests in their schooling should be focused on broad educational objectives and not on narrow therapeutic ones. They should, in other words, seek to deepen the current of interaction between a child's awareness of himself and his awareness of his world, and to broaden his channels of communication with classmates and teachers, while avoiding the exposure of emotional conflicts for purposes that are unrelated to curricular objectives. I think it important to emphasize this because of what I have found to be a typical first error made by many teachers who become persuaded that psychoanalytic principles can improve their teaching skills. Not content to lead their students to confront emotionally charged issues, they rush to interpret them in ways that are all too readily available in psychoanalytic case histories, overlooking that these are insight oriented, not outsight oriented, and therefore run contrary to the manifest purposes of teaching.

Let it be taken as a firm rule of thumb, therefore, that the sharing of dreams, daydreams, metaphors, and other products of preconscious processes should be encouraged as vehicles of communication and conceptualization—not as objects of clinical interpretation.

PRINCIPLE 9

As noted above, it is important that the children not perceive instructions in the expression of fantasies and feelings as encouragements to act them out in ways that would lead to anxiety. This precaution should not, however, be interpreted exclusively in terms of classroom management issues. The involvement of a child's responsible actions—as distinct from his occasional temptations to act out—can provide an important stabilizing base for the involvement in the learning process of his more personal thoughts, feelings, and images. This, again, is no more than to restate Bruner's interpretation of Piaget's findings that optimal learning involves the enactive mode of representing knowledge as well as the iconic and ratiocinative modes. Admittedly there are

some fine lines to be followed if the enactive mode is
to be invited into the educative process in ways that
avoid stimulation of psychonoxious impulses on the
one hand, and on the other hand the unrealities of
fun and games artifices. One way to steer this sensitive middle course is to involve the children themselves in appropriate teaching responsibilities from
the nursery school years on. This will require some
radical reexaminations of certain of our habitual assumptions regarding what can be learned without
benefit of professional teaching, and what it means to
be qualified to teach. Two self-evident truths may be
useful in undertaking these reexaminations: (1) Everyone has learned something that they could teach
to someone else. (2) The single best way to perfect
one's learning of anything is to teach it. There is
much room for experimentation in the application of
these truisms to routine issues of classroom protocol,
not only as they may pertain to the involvement of
fantasies and feelings but also as they may pertain to
long accepted procedures of cognitive drill and grill.
The assignment of some teaching responsibilities to
the children themselves in the areas to which this
presentation is addressed has, however, two special
considerations in its favor: (1) Young children usually have more to teach, i.e., are more expert in certain
aspects of the expression and use of fantasies and
feelings, than are most adults. (2) Real responsibilities for the well-being of other children are likely
to provide opportune vantage points from which to
develop reflexes of tact and courtesy in respect to
one's own emotional tender spots as well as to those
of others.

I am mindful that my presentation of these principles suffers from their not being concretely exemplified. This being impossible here I must be con-

tent with referring you, in addition to my own previous publications, to the writings of Barbara Ellis Long[8] of Saint Louis; George Brown[9] at the University of California at Santa Barbara; Robert Samples[10] and his colleagues at the Environmental Studies Project in Boulder, Colorado; Sheldon Roen of New York[11]; Terry Borton in the Philadelphia school system, whose recently published *Reach, Touch and Teach*[12] probably contains more examples of these principles than any book now in print; and, of course, Sylvia Ashton-Warner, author of *Spinster*[13] and *Teacher*[14], who knew instinctively what the rest of us had to learn. I omit George Dennison, John Holt, and Herbert Kohl only because their work is too well-known to need references from me.

PRINCIPLE 10

The teacher seeking to apply these principles should be guided by her sense of comfort before her sense of duty—at least until the two show signs of going together. Opportunities for innovation in these areas are too numerous for any teacher to take ad-

8. Barbara Ellis Long, "Using the Behavioral Sciences as a Focus for Social Studies: A String for the Beads," *Teaching Social Studies in Urban Schools* (Reading, Mass.: Addison-Wesley, 1971).
9. George Isaac Brown, *Human Teaching for Human Learning* (New York: Viking Press, 1971).
10. Robert Samples, "Toward the Intrinsic: A Plea for the Next Step in Curriculum," *The American Biology Teacher*, March, 1970.
11. Sheldon Roen, "The Behavioral Sciences in the Primary Grades," *American Psychologist*, 1965, 20.
12. Terry Borton, *Reach, Touch and Teach* (New York: McGraw-Hill, 1970).
13. Sylvia Ashton-Warner, *Spinster* (New York: Simon and Schuster, 1971).
14. Sylvia Ashton-Warner, *Teacher* (New York: Simon and Schuster, 1963).

vantage of. Any of the principles discussed above, which seek to make school more interesting and lively by engaging the children's natural feelings and images, will make for significant and visible gains, if applied in comfort and with confidence. There is no reason to apply all of them; indeed, there is good reason not to apply any of them uneasily. It is helpful, therefore, for teachers to have had some experience in exploring their own feelings before working with students on a feeling level. More and more schools of education are offering courses in "group process," "sensitivity groups," "humanistic psychology," or the like, where good training can be had under careful supervision. The National Training Laboratory, an associate of the National Education Association, 1201 Sixteenth Street, Northwest, Washington, D.C., 20036, conducts training sessions for all levels of school personnel. In addition, there are a number of "growth centers" or informal institutes where experienced leaders conduct short-term training sessions. A list of these centers can be obtained from the American Association of Humanistic Psychology, 584 Page Street, San Francisco, California, 94117.

I want to attach one disclaimer to these referrals. Many of these organizations and institutes are rallying around the term *affective education,* and this worries me. Because the term *affective education* conjures images of fruitless polemical haranguing between Affectivists and, I guess we would call them, Cognitionists. We should not allow such a polarization to take place. In support of that statement I call on no less knowledgeable a psychologist and no less reknowned a "cognitionist" than Jean Piaget who puts the matter thusly:

There is a constant parallel between the affective and intellectual life throughout childhood and adolescence. This statement will seem surprising only if one attempts to dichotomize the life of the mind into emotions and thoughts. But nothing could be more false or more superficial . . .

Of course affectivity is always the incentive for actions . . . since affectivity assigns value to activities and distributes energy to them. But affectivity is nothing without intelligence. Intelligence furnishes affectivity with its means and clarifies its ends. . . .

Intelligence thus begins neither with knowledge of the self nor of things as such but with knowledge of their interaction, and it is by orienting itself simultaneously toward the two poles of that interaction that intelligence organizes the world by organizing itself.[15]

Admittedly, we have seen too many educational experiments focus exclusively on the cultivation of cognitive skills. And it has doubtless been with resentful recognition of this exclusivism that some of the fresh new approaches coming to education from psychotherapy, from sensitivity training, from group dynamics, from meditation techniques and the like have invited a similar charge from the other side. But the central point to be drawn from Piaget's truism is not that exclusive attention to cognitive skills leaves something of value out of the educative process; the point is that such a singular focus results in bad cognitive education. Similarly, the point is not that experiments in affective education that leave curricular relevance to shift for itself are ignoring something of

15. John H. Flavell, *The Developmental Psychology of Jean Piaget,* (Princeton, New Jersey: Von Nostrand, 1963), p. 62.

value in the educative process; the point is that such experiments lead to bad affective education. Because, it bears repeating, "Intelligence . . . begins neither with knowledge of the self nor of things as such but with knowledge of their interaction."

What this means in educational terms is that we abuse a child just as much if we help him well in his development of self and then leave him to his own devices in linking that development to his enjoyment, creation, and remaking of culture—we abuse him just as much when we do that—as when we expect him to learn history, social studies, and other areas of commonly valued public knowledge apart from their relevance to his private world of personal concerns and interests. True, the latter abuse has been far more evident in American education than the former. But now, when at least some of us are beginning to be able to get this all together, let us not do what I did when I came to the last chapter. Let us not take our eye off the ball.

editor's comments

JONES ADDS his weight to the mounting swell of opinion against the artificial polarization of affect and cognition in education. In this instance, however, because of the writer's broad experience in individual and group psychotherapy, the point of view is even more significant. Here we have still another theorist—a specialist in the workings of the human mind—who believes that the failure to form a union between emotion and intellect will result only in further wasted motion.

Jones goes on to forewarn us that affect and cognition can lend themselves to both good and bad education.

What he is saying, I believe, is that we can choose to strive for cognitive and affective growth in clumsy and inept ways—or we can develop respectable techniques that have reasonable potency. In this regard, it would seem that because teaching that successfully integrates facts and feelings is still in its infancy, our greatest need is to invent a repertory of methods with which to integrate both domains.

It is equally significant that Jones is strongly opposed to education that allows excessive freedom. Both permissiveness and rigid authoritarianism, he says, can be replaced by some more desirable and more credible basis for authority. We find here, then, a second point of agreement between Jones and Maslow. Both believe that there is an optimum degree of freedom that should be made available to the child, and both agree that children vary in their ability to cope with freedom. We may infer from this one more criterion for individualizing instruction. Children differ not only in their learning styles and rates, but also in the amount of structure they require. I cannot help but note, at this point, that one of my own studies demonstrated rather conclusively that high-anxious children—children prone to anxiety—were limited in the amount of freedom they could tolerate. In contrast, children blessed with a high threshold for anxiety performed admirably in situations where there was a minimal amount of teacher-imposed control. Viewing this matter of classroom stress from the vantage point of instructional technique, Jones suggests that we would here be well-advised to guard against the kinds of role playing and acting out that lead to high levels of anxiety.

But anxiety is not in and of itself destructive; one of the chapter's more intriguing points is reflected in the writer's belief that a good curriculum problem should cause some emotional discomfort in the learner. Because teachers tend to fear any classroom activity that sets off an emotional threat, they generally restrict themselves to "safe" material—and, in so doing, reduce the child's intellectual diet to a state of extreme blandness. One suspects that much of the boredom that characterizes so many classrooms comes from such efforts at curricular safety.

From the standpoint of constructive change, it seems to me that Jones's postulation provides two clues for educational leadership: first, through programs of continuing education, teachers must learn how to involve children's feelings and at the same time prevent the expression of these feelings from progressing to the acting out stage; and, second, teachers must gain a sufficiently sophisticated grasp of their own subject matter so that they can relate it to the entire range of human feelings and symbolism.

In his discussion of this last point, Jones indirectly comments upon an ancient dispute regarding the relative importance of teaching technique and knowledge of subject matter. Despite his tremendous concern for the affective side of education, Jones believes that, for example, it is the teacher with a rich fund of cognitive knowledge that best is able to relate facts and feelings. In another chapter, Bloom reaches essentially the same conclusion—from a different route—when he notes that healthy emotions are closely linked with cognitive success.

There are further elements of common agreement that can be noted between this and the other chapters. Jones shares Eisner's conviction that forms of nonverbal symbolization—such as painting, music, and drama—must receive far more attention than currently is the case. Like Scriven he believes that, instead of inflicting our pet meanings upon children, we must help them to find their own. He concurs, further, with my own impression that emotional learning must not be separated from cognitive goals. He wants a greater connection between the classroom and the world outside: like Meade, he feels that education should "seek to deepen the current of interaction between a child's awareness of himself and his awareness of his world." Finally, by implication, Jones underscores Tyler's persuasion that teacher retraining is crucial, for the brand of education described in the chapter will require a collection of teaching techniques that go well beyond those currently in use.

One other aspect of the chapter is, I think, worthy of special mention. A decade ago, creativity was in high fashion as a curriculum goal. During the early part of the decade just past, a number of excellent studies by Getzels, Jackson, McKinnon, and others were published. A central thesis of these studies was the notion that all humans have a capacity for creative endeavor, and that the expression and use of this capacity was highly satisfying. Although creativity has now lost some of its high fashion in educational literature, the importance of creative self-expression now has, it seems to me, a new kind of relevance. For not only does the expression of one's creative impulses seem to fit neatly with arguments on the importance of symbolic activity, but it also provides an attractive device for rekindling the child's sense of personal involvement. It may be, consequently, that the emphasis on creativity is deserving of a fresh revival.

8.

At best our conception of intelligence is a restricted one. Learning in the present school is largely a matter of verbalisms. Hence, for the capable but non-verbal child, the odds of educational failure are very great. We need, consequently, to reexamine what it is that we mean by intelligence, and to reexplore the child's great potential for learning that does not depend on words.

chapter 8

THE INTELLIGENCE
OF FEELING

Elliot W. Eisner

IT IS TESTIMONY to the dynamism of American educational life that this volume should be published. After all, it was not too long ago that the watchword in American schools was "get tough," upgrade the curriculum by providing a diet of really intellectually rigorous content, do not coddle, schools are for learning and for producing what society needs for maintaining its political and economic position in the world. To be sure, these views are not now wholly rejected, although they have, I believe, softened considerably. But more importantly, a new wave, one that was born a few years ago, is only now beginning to hit our shores. American educators, taking their lead from the youth of the world, are becoming sensitized to the affective side of life and its place in the experience of schooling. This book is only one piece of evidence of that fact.

During the mid-1950s, the emphasis that pervaded educational literature was cognitive in character, especially after Sputnik's rise on 4 October 1957. Such an emphasis was, of course, consistent with an intellectual heritage that for generations had separated affect from intellect. That tradition, stemming from Plato's distinctions between the life of feeling and the life of thought, provided the bedrock upon which so much educational practice has been based. The common-sense distinctions that are made between thought and emotion, between the theoretical and the practical, between the vocational and the professional, between working with one's hand and working with one's head can be traced to a Greek tradition at least twenty-three hundred years old. Thus, when the pressures fell upon schoolmen to intellectualize the school by exorcising whatever remnants remained—real or fancied—of progressive education, such pressures had the support of tradition. Combined with our hypersensitivity to the Russian achievement in space and our national need to find a reason, the schools bore the brunt of the attack. Although critics of American public education had been lambasting schoolmen for at least a decade prior to Sputnik, it was this achievement that coalesced the social forces necessary for making important curricular changes in educational programs. And how did those changes come about? There was no doubt at that time that not only the softness of schooling needed to be stiffened, but that the best way to do it was by a piecemeal approach to curriculum reform. There was hardly a doubt in anyone's mind that the curriculum, subject by subject, should be reformed by using scholars from the disciplines to provide the leadership and teachers from the schools to provide whatever practical know-how the scholars did not possess. Educational reform was conceived of as curriculum reform. Curriculum reform was thought of as developing programs that more closely approximated college and university courses in the various academic fields.

Times change, however, and the past fifteen years have been ones of radical change, not only in America but throughout the world. To my mind, the most dramatic of such changes are those found in the ways the young look at life and the ways in which they choose to live it. High school and college students of two decades ago were on the whole an obsequious lot, more often concerned with seeing how many freshmen could be stuffed into a telephone booth than with how the poor could be fed. Of course, there were groups of students actively engaged in social action, but for the most part such students were an exception to the vast majority who wanted to make it to the suburbs to live the life of peace and plenty.

When an institution has "clients" who view its services as necessary and desirable ingredients for a full and successful life, the institution's ability to function with near autonomy is quite great. The dependency of the student breeds an institutional cockiness that many institutions displayed a decade ago, and besides, if students didn't behave, there was always the draft and the Korean "conflict." Times *have* changed.

Today we are less sure than we were a decade ago about how to improve educational practice. A decade ago monolithic solutions seemed obvious. I believe we have begun to learn (although it is a lesson that the history of education could have taught us) that educational answers are always time bound and contextual in character. Furthermore, those of us in education are facing a student population that as often as not does not give a damn about the values that motivated us during our own high school and college years. Students today—not all to be sure, but a substantial proportion—are seeing life in terms different from our own and are forcing us to reexamine what schools are for and what roles we might play within them. Perhaps most significant is the growing interest in the life of feeling, with personal identity, with listening to your own drummer. These characteristics of youthful attitudes were, of course, initiated well before the current revolution began by writers and artists such as Jack Kerouac, and E.E. Cummings. These men told us through their works what was ahead; they were the granddaddies of *Midnight Cowboy* and *Easy Rider*. But American educators seldom take their lead from the arts; after all, how much confidence can be placed in fiction?

So today, we try to come to grips with a new mode of thought about education. Today we try to attend to the affective side of educational practice, to expand our theories, theories that are focused upon achievement in cognitive terms, in order to cope with a movement that many of us feel we cannot and should not ignore.

I cannot help but wonder whether the new realization and our efforts to deal with its insistent demands is a form of coping behavior that stems from a radically altered view of education or whether it is a veneer that we have temporarily applied to ourselves in order to ride on and not drown in the waves about us. Whether the former or the latter, I do not believe we can succeed unless we develop more comprehensive conceptions of mind than those we have and use at present. This will require us to unload some of the theoretical baggage that we have grown accustomed to carrying around. I would like to identify some of the baggage and to put forward some ideas about human intelligence that have already been adumbrated by Maslow and Jones in this volume.

Perhaps the heaviest intellectual burden that we need to relinquish is the one that dichotomizes affect and intellect. Now it is a convenience to conceive of minds operating in compartments, each of which has particular functions, and then to identify which of these compartments schooling shall have responsibility for. It is, of course, a theoretical convenience, indeed a necessity, to analyze and to make distinctions that focus attention and refine conception. But when conceptual distinctions are reified, and then operationalized in curricular hierarchies, we carry distinctions beyond their usefulness; affect and intellect are examples. Affect, in the eyes of many in education, deals with feeling, and feelings are not intellectual functions. Intellect, on the other hand, is associated with cognition, and cognition deals with understanding, and hence with thought. In spite of the fact that cognition originally referred to that process through which the organism becomes aware of its environment, cognition has come to mean linguistically mediated thought; indeed, some people actually believe that thought can only be carried by the vehicle of discursive language.

The educational ramifications of such a belief, especially one as embedded and pervasive as this one, are enormous. Its meanings for schooling are several. First, it means that those content areas that are linguistically saturated will be dominant in the curriculum. If intellect is associated with verbal discourse, and if the school is responsible for developing intellect, it is clear that those fields of human activity where linguistic performance dominates, will also dominate the curriculum. And this, of course, is precisely what has occurred. There are precious few schools in which even parity between nondiscursive and discursive fields occur in educational programs. Music, dance, drama, film making, the areas of drawing, painting, and even poetry and other artful uses of language are seldom given serious attention in schools. Part of the reason for their neglect is due to our implicit and covert belief that such fields are not intellectual; they have little to do with the use or development of mind.

Second, because the content areas that constitute the major parts of the curriculum are linguistically saturated, and in part because of the tradition to which teachers were exposed as children, the methods used for instruction are similarly highly verbal in nature. Thus, students whose aptitudes for learning utilize other modalities are, in effect, penalized by the parochial and limited instructional modes that dominate teaching in American schools. Bloom's comments about the need for using a variety of instructional modes so as not to penalize children whose linguistic aptitudes are limited is well taken. Unfortunately, most of the new curricula pay little attention to this problem.

Third, the circumscription of discursive language with thought has tended to penalize students whose strengths and interests are in other areas of human action. Thus, the student who would rather dance or paint than study German, French, or chemistry is often viewed as intellectually inferior. The labels, the expectations, and the programs that are provided for such students often make entry into college difficult. Our view of intellect as verbally mediated thought penalizes those whose talents or interests lie elsewhere and creates a self-fulfilling prophecy that reassures us of the correctness of our original view. We have not yet begun to take seriously the idea that man's symbolic processes are wider than his discourse and that to limit man's education to what can be said is to restrict, at least as far as schools are concerned, what he is capable of knowing and ex-

pressing. Indeed, a host of contemporary philosophers such as Michael Polanyi, Herbert Read, Susanne Langer, and Murice Merleau-Ponty have
pointed this out in their writings, but ideas such as
the ones they have developed have not squared with
the positivistic orientation to knowledge that has
dominated for so long our conception of what knowledge is and the methods through which it is secured.

I am arguing, therefore, that the serious revision of
school programs will require relinquishing some concepts and beliefs that have become familiar terms in
thought about education. But the giving up of familiar but dysfunctional conceptions of mind and educational practice will not by itself bring about a conception of education more adequate. I will in this paper
sketch a conception of intelligence that appears to
me to describe more adequately the intellectual processes dealing with the creation and appreciation of
affective life. What I will do is to argue that the
production and appreciation of objects, events,
images, and relationships among men are subject to
the controls exercised by human intelligence, and as
such are capable of being expanded through appropriate experience. Because the subject matter of such
experience and the use of such intelligence, especially
in those forms we normally associate with the arts,
are qualitative in character, this mode of intellectual
functioning can be called *qualitative intelligence.* In
using this term I take the lead that John Dewey provided in a generally neglected chapter of his book,
Philosophy and Civilization,[1] published in 1931. In
this chapter, titled "Qualitative Thought," Dewey
tried to identify those aspects of thinking that are

1.   John Dewey, *Philosophy and Civilization* (New York: Minton,
Balch and Co., 1931).

borne with and by qualities. It was later, however, in *Art as Experience*,[2] published three years after *Philosophy and Civilization* and his last major work, that Dewey stressed in unambiguous terms the role of intelligence in artistic action. Dewey wrote:

> Any idea that ignores the necessary role of intelligence in production of works of art is based upon identification of thinking with use of one special kind of material, verbal signs and words. To think effectively in terms of relations of qualities is as severe a demand upon thought as to think in terms of symbols, verbal and mathematical. Indeed, since words are easily manipulated in mechanical ways, the production of a work of genuine art probably demands more intelligence than does most of the so-called thinking that goes on among those who pride themselves on being "intellectuals."[3]

In describing the role of intelligence in the production of art, Dewey did not mean to imply that the arts were something removed from life and altogether special in character. To the contrary, the roots of the arts are to be found in the day-to-day relationships that man creates between himself and his environment, including his fellow man. This generous view of art and broad conception of mind did not assign feeling to a lower intellectual level and thought to a higher one, for thought is a necessary ingredient in things felt. In order to create human relationships that are civil and humane, the qualities constituting such relationships must be selected and organized; they must be reordered dynamically when

2. John Dewey, *Art as Experience* (New York: Minton, Balch and Co., 1934).
3. Ibid., p. 46.

quantities in the environment change. Thus, a teacher, for example, must be able to experience (be sensitive to, we say) the qualities displayed by his students and must be able to create qualities through his actions that contribute to a humane, civil, and educational environment. Think for a moment what this means in the act of teaching. It means that the teacher will be able to experience and understand the meaning of the vast array of qualitative cues provided by the group or individual with which he works. Furthermore, he must have some end in view that enables him to select, as it were, a particular array of qualities that will move the state of affairs in a direction considered educationally valuable. To do this, he not only needs to be able to experience the aforementioned cues, he also needs to be able to conceive of and create through his own actions the appropriate display of other qualities. When a teacher does this well, we are likely to describe his teaching as artful. We may say his tempo, his pacing, his rapport with students is keen. When we see such behavior, we rightfully admire it because we ourselves are moved by the pedagogical versatility that the teacher displays. His actions for us become a minor work of art.

One analogue to the qualitative intelligence displayed by the teacher is found in the work of the stand-up comedian. He too is before a group in a state of flux. He too provides and responds to a flow of qualities, qualities that cannot always be predicted. To survive on stage the comedian must be able to understand, in qualitative terms, the meaning of the qualities displayed by his audience. When to speed up the pace, when to slow it down, how much time to allow to elapse before the punch line; these decisions are not deduced from a psychological theory of behavior but rather from a highly developed and re-

fined qualitative intelligence that allows qualities to
be experienced in the first place, and a repertoire of
qualitatively loaded actions from which the comedian
can draw.

The analogy of the comedian to the teacher is not
meant to imply that teachers should aspire to be
comics or that all of the functions of the teacher can
be subsumed under those of the comedian. The analogue was drawn to illustrate one of the ways in
which qualitative intelligence is exercised in each of
the roles.

It would also be unfortunate if the impression were
left that qualitative intelligence is exercised only in
some aspects of teaching and in comedy. On the contrary, qualitative intelligence is exercised whenever
qualities are selected, organized, and experienced in
whatever areas of life one functions within. How we
choose to dress, the style with which we express our
thoughts, the environment we create in the homes in
which we live are products of qualitative thought. To
take a trivial example, women understand especially
well the appropriate use of make-up for different
social situations. The eyeliner just a wee bit too long
or the eye shadow just a bit too dark alters a face
from one that was appropriate for the office to one
more appropriate for a cocktail party. In countless
ways the selection and rejection of qualities are made
as we function in life.

The classroom and the school of which it is a part
also display a pervasive quality that results from the
choices made by students and teachers within it.
Whether the classroom is formal and stiff, or informal and flexible, is a product of choices made by
those who live in it. The terms *stiff* and *flexible* are,
of course, metaphors. They describe what we sense
about places. After all, a piece of cardboard can be

stiff and a piece of wire flexible in fact, but hardly a classroom or a school. Yet our use of metaphor provides telling evidence of our awareness of the qualities that characterize human situations. We say, for example, that relationships are warm or cold, that people are smooth or coarse, that situations are taut or slack. When such metaphors are used, they reveal in their aptness our perception of the pervasive quality of the event and our ability to find, not a linguistic equivalent, but a poetic analogue that renders and thus communicates the central quality of the event to others. Perhaps nowhere is this mode of intelligence used in greater measure than in the creation of poetry and literature.

I believe that our current interest in the affective or experiential aspects of schooling is a result of our neglect of the qualities that we have inadvertently created in many of our schools. Our students are telling us that schools are impersonal, bureaucratic, and unresponsive to them as people; in a word, they are cold. American educators have tried to improve the quality of education by improving the curriculum of the schools and by developing or adapting instructional approaches used in industrial and military settings. We have, in our effort to increase both effectiveness and efficiency, utilized tools and made choices that, in relation to a planning grid, made systematic sense. There is some utility in viewing the school as a factory and education as an industry. Almost any root metaphor will provide some useful perspective from which to look at an enterprise. But I believe that our metaphors have been much too circumscribed. In viewing schooling from a technological perspective we have neglected the qualitative consequences of decisions made using such a model. Thus, if teachers are viewed as educational engineers, then students are likely to be seen as raw material to be engineered. In our desire to eliminate educational waste and to insure that the school will be efficiently managed, thus avoiding the charge of running a loose shop, we have, I believe, failed to appreciate the qualitative ramifications of the countless bureaucratic decisions that have been made. Whether they be in the form of testing, grading, tracking, or the use of the timetable—these decisions begin to develop a critical mass that alters the pervasive quality of the school as a whole. Such altered qualities in turn begin to affect how people behave within the institution. Thus the pervasive quality of the school becomes a type of qualitative control affecting the character of the qualities that are considered appropriate within the institution. Think for a moment how the austerity of some libraries almost forces one to hush one's voice, or to walk across the floor as though it were made of raw eggs still in their shells.

Many students of organizational environment have described classrooms and schools in terms of the atmosphere they display. Whithall, Lewin, Halpin and Croft, and Pace and Stern are only a few who could be mentioned. What has generally been neglected is the realization that the qualities that characterize the classroom, school, indeed any social situation, can in principle be altered through the exercise of qualitative intelligence. Some men earn their living by creating qualitative environments; we call such men interior designers. Others work on an even larger scale; we call them city planners. What I believe we must recognize is that the qualities that affect our lives are those that are not only built into our physical surroundings, but also in the ways in which we relate to others. Further, we must recognize that what looks like a purely administrative consideration can have profound qualitative consequences. We have not been in the habit of anticipating the ripple effect of the decisions we make. What looks like a convenience from one angle can turn out to be a nuisance of the first order from another perspective. We did not anticipate when highways were built between the suburbs and the central city how long the traffic jams were going to be or how long fathers would be kept away from their families. The quality of life is in large measure a spin-off of such neglect.

Thus far in this paper I have tried to make several points. One of these is that in America we are witnessing a growing shift in our orientation to the means and ends of education. I have argued further that this shift has in large measure been stimulated by the young as a result of our neglect of the qualities pervading both the schools and the social order generally. I have pointed out that if we are to improve educational practice in a direction that is more humane and that genuinely appreciates and attempts to develop the potential that differentiates men from each other, we will need to give up some of the concepts that characterize our thought about mind and education. One such dysfunctional term is the distinction we make between thought and feeling.

Further, I have argued that while the elimination of useless or hampering concepts is a beginning, it is clearly inadequate; what I believe we need is a new conception, one that unifies dichotomies and makes them more useful for educational practice. The conception I have described is the concept of qualitative intelligence, a notion that makes it possible to conceive of the ability to create or appreciate qualitative work as one subject to educational intervention.

It must be obvious that to intervene adequately in

order to bring about the changes I have described a variety of changes will need to be made in the schools. If we expand our conception of mind and recognize the intellectual aspects of qualitative thought, we will be more likely to be able to expand the range of educational options available to students. Our priorities at present, as far as curriculum content is concerned, are based partly on our conception of intellect, partly on tradition, and partly on the realistic realization that only certain competencies will be rewarded by the academic gatekeepers to higher education. Parents understandably believe that school programs ought not to jeopardize their children's chances for college and university entrance or for social or economic mobility. As long as academic programs are defined in the ways they are at present, and as long as high-level performance in such programs is a prerequisite for college, the likelihood of reordering priorities in schooling and of increasing the range of educational options available to students is slight.

When schools are viewed as the major social mechanisms that sort out the more able from the less able —something like a giant sieve—the practice of holding curriculum content constant across students and then selecting a certain percentage of the "winners" can easily be justified. Indeed, differentiation of school programs would simply make the task of picking out the academically able more difficult. A common race with common hurdles is far easier.

If, however, schools are viewed as resources that a society provides to its citizens not only to pass on the culture but to develop their particular talents, to follow and develop their particular interests, to—as Maslow has said—self-actualize, then the range of guided inquiries that schools ought to make possible will become quite diverse. Increasingly, as children use the school as one of the vehicles available for their educational development, the sorts of studies, projects, and issues with which they deal will be of their own formation. In such a view the mission of the school is not primarily one of selection but one of education—the conscious, purposeful effort to expand human intelligence. Will we be able to develop such a view of the school's mission, or are we destined to continue to use schools as a continually narrowing road that near its end only has room for a few to pass through?

It is also clear that if the content of school programs is to have utility in the social world the problems that pervade social life will need attention. Both Meade and Scriven have provided telling examples of the ways in which schools avoid such problems. By eviscerating curricula of emotional content and controversial issues we have left a remainder so bland as to make engagement difficult. Scriven has identified some of the issues that need attention and Meade has pointed out some of the educational virtues of confrontation. The general thrust of both of their papers I support. But I cannot help but wonder whether communities are likely to allow schools to encourage students to examine closely and question the values that now operate in social life. Will communities be willing to take such risks or, put another way, can one expect the public to understand what education is for?

Not only the content but the methods of school programs need examination and revision. Both Bloom and Jones have addressed themselves to this issue. Their observations and recommendations are at the level of principle, and we desperately need in the classroom particular pedagogical procedures that

teachers can employ to stimulate and develop qualitative thought. Role playing, the use of the visual and
the dramatic arts, the use of new types of media that
communicate through modalities other than the verbal need development. Jones's observation that fan-
tasizing should be routine in school, a familiar part
of the classroom culture, is in my opinion both in-
sightful and apt. Why should this valuable asset of
human consciousness be seen as an appendix to a
larger body? Why shouldn't schools encourage children to dream, to envision, to speculate? Those who
refuse to speculate, wrote Alfred North Whitehead,
are traitors to the future. To what degree do schools
inhibit such processes by penalizing failure and by
encouraging the avoidance of risk?

Finally, I believe that schools must attend to the
general attitudes and dispositions that they are developing in the young regarding their own sense of personal adequacy and their own ability to inquire. For
too many students today's schools are essentially an
array of meaningless hurdles that they learn they can
never adequately leap over. As Tyler has pointed out,
such students continue to "fail" and eventually drop
out. For the so-called culturally disadvantaged student the consequences of schooling are dramatic. For
such students the dropout rate in high school approaches 65 percent. But while not as dramatic for
the middle-class student, the chorelike, intellectually
feckless quality of schooling can create attitudes that
are just as deleterious. What would we do to schools
if we wanted to make them really intellectually vital
places to which students would flock? How would we
change the relationship we now establish with students? What changes in school programs would
occur? In what ways would our use of space and material differ? How would we go about assessing the

programs we provided and how would we provide feedback to those involved? In dealing with such questions it is apparent that a wide, indeed a comprehensive, approach to educational reform would need to be undertaken. Piecemeal approaches are likely to drown in the sea in which they are thrown. But while we do not yet have adequate answers, we are now able to raise some of the questions. And as Dewey once said, a well-posed question is half the answer. Let us hope we can find the other half before the questions change.

editor's comments

EISNER ARGUES, perhaps more explicitly than any of the other writers, that the changing times demand a radically altered view of education. The implication is that—as the society continues its inexorable evolution—our schools are increasingly better suited to the past than to the future. In point of fact, the chapter documents problems that have become a good deal more critical in the last decade—the need to provide all children with a quality education, and thus to compensate for limitations in preschool experience, peculiarities in learning style, bilingualism, reading disability, emotional handicaps, and other pranks of fate that victimize children.

The matters that concern Eisner are, as he notes, reflected in the spate of curricular tinkering that has arisen recently. "Free" schools have been started, at least in part, to overcome excessive authoritarianism; open schools have been created so that learning could take place more naturally; programs for individualizing instruction have been designed so that the psychological idiosyncrasies of children might be better accommodated; black history has been introduced in the hope that children from a deprived minority might not be denied their cultural heritage; and there presently is a fresh, new movement to reduce the competitiveness that is so characteristic of life in school.

Now we are directed by Eisner to still another defect. Our present conception of intellect, he says, is preponderantly associated with verbal discourse; because verbalism dominates the curriculum, and because most instruction is thus heavily dependent upon verbal facility, nonverbal students are placed at a great and unjustifiable disadvantage.

It is apparent, moreover, that the author questions the appropriateness of the existing curriculum for even high-verbal students. Our present approach to instruction denies the child adequate opportunity to sense, to feel, and to express himself. In this regard, I believe the fault lies in assuming that because verbalism was good enough for our grandfathers, it should be equally good for our grandsons. The world *does* alter itself, and a half-century of social development is likely to produce, in the natural course of events, vast personality differences between grandfather and grandson. These differences, quite obviously, may—in addition to a changed outlook on life—reflect a greater passion for both self-expression and nonverbal expression. Eisner reminds us that we have an unfortunate habit of assuming that if a child cannot ventilate his feelings through words, he must not feel. The point is not wholly absurd; the teacher who judges his students solely on the basis of what they write and say in class is not uncommon. It is for this reason, I suspect, that he is moved to comment upon the inhospitable quality of school life.

We are asked, therefore, to give consideration to a different concept of intelligence—one that provides connecting links between words and the thoughts and the feelings they symbolize. Such a curriculum is not prohibitive. The chief requirements are those of increasing the opportunity for nonverbal learning experiences, and of estimating the child's learning needs through a greater abundance of nonverbal procedures. If, in other words, we give children more of a chance to sense, to feel, and to react, we can then evaluate the yield from such self-expression, and—on this evidence—determine the kinds of school experiences they most need. It is interesting to note, on this account, that procedures of this sort are customarily applied where children's recreation and play are concerned, but for some reason we have considered them inapplicable to schooling.

The shape of the reconstruction Eisner envisions is defined by the disabilities that give rise to our present condition: "Our priorities at present, as far as curriculum content is concerned, are based partly on our conception of intellect, partly on tradition, and partly on the realistic realization that only certain competencies will be rewarded by the academic gatekeepers to higher education." The necessary remedies, consequently, follow by implication: we need, in one way or another, to interrupt practices that are merely traditional, to reconsider the meaning of intelligence and intellect, and to revise the schedule of qualifications that permits a student to enter the college or university.

Eisner points out, for example, that at least in the case of the college-bound student the present entrance requirements must be modified before the secondary school curriculum can be shifted. Because these requirements are at best arbitrary and at worst capricious, there is nothing to prevent the reform from taking place at once. It is, in fact, already underway, having become somewhat of a minor movement among small liberal arts colleges.

The matters of habit and tradition, on the other hand, are somewhat more of a puzzlement. It is doubtful whether most parents can ever be persuaded that a rich imaginal life and healthy emotions (attributes that are difficult to demonstrate tangibly) are a fitting substitute for knowledgeability. As a result, it is likely that we will find it necessary to accomplish at least a majority of the school's current cognitive objectives with greater dispatch, thus freeing time for attention to affect and symbolism. But, if Carl Rogers is correct, emotional growth of necessity facilitates both cognitive achievement and learning efficiency. Hence, greater emphasis upon emotion may, in the long run, prove to be a step toward heightened efficiency.

The third of Eisner's suggested changes—a conception of intelligence and intellect that includes the individual's affective and symbolic life—finds its answer, once again, in the retraining of teachers and in the development of new kinds of instructional lessons.

To be sure, the arts, as Eisner, Maslow, and Jones say, have been sadly neglected. To make matters worse, what little attention has been given has focused essentially on performance skills rather than on sensory response. One hunches, however, that Eisner's intent goes well beyond the arts themselves: if we are to have education that is more humane—which genuinely values and nurtures the potential that distinguishes men from one another—we will need to relinquish some of the formulations that characterize our thought about mind and education. While compelled to attend school, every child ought to have a rich and endless opportunity to develop whatever inherent gifts he has. These gifts go far beyond the ability to pass an examination—they incorporate the entire range of human talent. Put another way, we need a curriculum that not only teaches children to think, but that also teaches them to feel, sense, appreciate, and enjoy, as well.

9.

The needed reform is complicated by the fact that the citizenry worships different educational ideologies. At bottom, however, each of these ideologies is directed toward the cultivation of a successful human. The movement to reform, consequently, must allow for alternative paths to the good life.

chapter 9

THE ENVIRONMENT
OF SCHOOLING
Louis J. Rubin

WE HAVE READ, in the preceding chapters, a comprehensive criticism of the present educational system. The indictments that have been expressed cover a large front: students have too little control over their own educational destiny; the normal confrontations of group life are eliminated in deference to an artificial serenity; the child's imaginal life has been largely ignored; we have failed to integrate the learnings that occur in and out of school; a ready-made value system that often conflicts with youth's sense of the world has been imposed tyranically; we have made insufficient use of what is known about learning and have thus been unable to ensure cognitive mastery; and, above all, we have neglected to infuse the school environment itself with either excitement, joy, or satisfaction. Pieced together, these criticisms provide both a diagnosis of the system's ills and a prescription for change.

Such prescriptions, unhappily, are not easily filled. One need not wholly agree with the writers to acknowledge that virtually anything now going on in the schools—as in our other institutions—can be done better. The need for massive change is therefore undeniable. But traditions die a slow death and need does not always beget action. Although the present system already manifests the unmistakable signs of old age, and its infirmities threaten to do us in, people are reluctant to part with the past. The education professions, for example, have diligently pursued significant change for more than a decade. Yet their accomplishments to date are much less than impressive. The reasons for this failure are many. For one thing, there is far more agreement about the problems than about the correctives. More energy has therefore been devoted to debate than to the initiation of solutions. Moreover, because the schools are an extraordinarily large business, they are subject to endless manipulation. Instances in which the child's best interests are undermined by what is politically expedient are anything but rare. Apathy, too, is a factor: a majority of parents, unaware of alternative approaches to education, either fail to take advantage of political opportunities to make their expectations and concerns known to school authorities, or defer to the will of minority factions laboring special prejudices. Further, the political realities of the society being what they are, the gains of the winners are enhanced by the losses of the losers. To wit, schooling is the primary entry point for the more desirable, hence lucrative, vocations. Thus, academic failure serves to reduce the vocational options of many students, limiting the number of qualified applicants for a desirable job, and increasing the probability of success among those who do survive the educational competition. Many desperately needed changes, in short, may not benefit those who, in one way or another, are now able to compensate for the system's deficiencies.

More than anything else, however, the improvement of our present system is complicated by the vast difference in opinion as to the purpose of schooling. Virtually no one is opposed to public education. Most people want more, rather than less, for their children. But there is an astonishing dissension regarding what schools are for, and what constitutes a good education. For some parents, pride in ethnic identity is the crucial goal in their children's education. Football, for some, is virtually a way of life, and for others, it is an insufferable waste. One father prides a son who can fathom advanced mathematics, whereas another is more interested in the ability to earn enough money to buy a home calculator or hire a bookkeeper. Such conflicts in attitude are all too well-known. Throughout the history of the school, we have expected parents with atypical points of view to accede to whatever seemed to best serve the majority. In days gone by, most were philosophically content to do so. We have come, however, to that point in the society's evolution where the expectations of the majority are increasingly disparate, and the needs of particular minorities more and more pointed. These needs, it is interesting to note, are not always educational in nature. The bitter issues of control, bussing, and school finance, for example, have not dealt with the curriculum or with teaching method, but rather with the political elements of the educational enterprise.

Of even greater moment, however, the inexorable force of the minor social revolutions now underway, making old customs and values no longer workable, and creating a hopeless hunger for a life-style that can never again be, have generated a public passion for any cure-all that has even minimal seductive appeal. Thus faddism abounds. We are in the midst of "open" and "free" schools, ghetto universities, storefront learning centers, voucher plans, and a host of other well-intentioned but improbable solutions to the educational dilemma. Despite the unlikeliness of their long-range success, however, a serendipitous blessing has emerged, for the public has reached an unprecedented willingness to experiment with new kinds of educational endeavors.

The time for legitimate and far-reaching change, therefore, has never been more ripe. Rather than pursue ends that are stillborn, consequently, it may be that we can best take advantage of the present confusion by taking a hard look at the kinds of human skills our changing society is likely to require.

SOME PRELIMINARY SUPPOSITIONS

In setting forth some notions regarding the nature of these skills, I shall attempt to draw upon the points made earlier in the volume. It is possible, I believe, to synthesize many of these arguments into a reasonably comprehensive pattern. Conjoined with some convictions of my own, the pattern may provide a rudimentary outline of a new sort of curriculum, one addressed to a pluralistic educational system, yielding a variety of options for its customers.

I have used several suppositions as a point of departure. Among these is the belief that the majority of the criticisms that have been expressed are just, and that a profound reform is needed. There is, after all, nothing startling about the fact that our children may need a different kind of school than we ourselves required a decade or two ago. The assumption that men can devise a school that will serve equally well in all seasons is one of the great educational myths with which we are still afflicted. Schools mirror the societies in which they exist, and alternations in one necessitate corresponding adjustments in the other.

Another supposition has to do with the inseparability of curriculum and educational purpose. We cannot, in other words, speak of educational strengths and weaknesses without reference to the end goals we seek. One generation may hold the school accountable for the production of plumbers and surgeons, another may ask it to produce individuals with a vast storehouse of information at their intellectual fingertips, and a third may demand that the schools develop people who are psychologically intact. Each generation, therefore, will require a different kind of school.

Still another supposition follows naturally: educational change, the transition from one kind of school to another, is an infinitely more complex phenomenon than we have heretofore suspected. Indeed, judging from the experience of the last dozen or so years, the discovery and perfection of the improvements themselves may well be the simplest of the required steps. If an authentic innovation is to be truly successful, the consumer must understand both the disabilities of the old way and the benefits of the new. Schoolmen have learned the hard way that an uninformed public often grows suspicious, uncooperative, and, in time, rebellious. Beyond all this, teachers must be retrained, students must learn to function in a new system, and the institutional bureaucracy itself must be bent into an appropriate new shape.

The outline derived from these suppositions, set forth in the last three chapters of the volume, is of several parts: first, some preliminary postulations that, collectively, fashion a kind of rationale; next, a description of some essential changes; and, lastly, a consideration of the pitfalls inherent in the changeover—the necessary communication with the public at large, the required reorganization, and the indispensable element of professional retraining.

SOME RESULTING POSTULATIONS

Let us begin then with three postulations. First, assume, if only in the interest of speculation, that the purpose of education is that of developing successful humans. Second, assume that successful humans are those who can cope with their life problems, find satisfaction and occasional joy in their life pursuits, and in some way contribute to the welfare of their society. Third, assume that because man comes in different shapes and forms, the development of successful humans will require not one, but a variety of educational prescriptions. One, of course, may choose to quarrel, semantically or theoretically, with any one or all three of these postulations. It seems probable, however, that their actualization would almost certainly lead to a better school system than the one we now have.

To expand briefly upon the first of the three postulations, when we take the purpose of education to be the cultivation of successful humans, we can allow for individual difference in nature and need, and avoid most of the ancient disputes about what subject matter is of most worth. We may choose to teach the student physics, art, or French, or we may permit him to select learning tasks of his own choosing, questing for knowledge that has personal appeal, or we may allow such decisions to evolve out of a cooperative alliance between student and teacher. But in each instance our primary concern is the development of a successful human—one able to accommodate the demands of his circumstance. The mastery of a particular intellectual idea or the realization of a particular emotional state thus assume a secondary importance. Dewey wrote:

> Knowledge is humanistic in quality not because it is *about* human products in the past, but because of what it *does* in liberating human intelligence and human sympathy. Any subject matter which accomplishes this result is humane, and any subject matter which does not accomplish it is not even educational.[1]

When we set our sights on this larger view of education we reduce the danger of confusing means with ends. The child's unique gifts serve as the point of departure and their progressive development as the ultimate goal. It is the evolution of the child himself, therefore, and not the conventions of the society, nor the aspirations of his parents, nor the blandishments of the educational hucksters, nor the theories of the philosophers, that must prevail. Because humans are not made successful by knowledge or feeling or even accomplishment alone, it is the balanced mix among these that matters most. The learner must acquire enough of man's accumulated wisdom to cope with the social, economic, and moral problems he will encounter in the time ahead; he must learn to separate what has real meaning and significance from that which is only trivial; he must come to understand what can be done with the proper use of his powers of intelligence; and he must reach for the inner tranquility that is the by-product of a stable set of emotions—but these things can be worked at in an infinite variety of ways. And, of even greater consequence, none is sufficient unto itself; each is an

1. John Dewey, *Democracy and Education* (New York: Macmillan Co., 1916), p. 269.

indispensable part in the makeup of a healthy person. Achieving one at the expense of another will only perpetuate our present disabilities.

Turning now to the second of our three postulations, if successful people are individuals who can deal effectively with their life situations, some new questions arise. If children come to school with different psychological needs and different intellectual tastes, should the school not be flexible to cater to these variations? More, should not the experiences of schooling themselves be exercises in success rather than failure? And, finally, if our aim is that of nurturing the ability to cope, should we not look to essential life skills rather than to what Whitehead called inert knowledge, or to humanistic charades as the basis for a curriculum?

Where in the present curriculum, it may be asked, do we provide learning that mitigates against violence, the culture of drugs, or psychological depression? Where do we guard against the possibility that precious talent may lie fallow throughout the length of a person's days? Where do we compensate for a child's socially induced sense of inadequacy and worthlessness? And where in the curriculum do we enable the student to learn about himself and to become the kind of person he wants to be?

Schools are less embracing than their patrons suppose. It is often assumed, for example, that adult actions are the natural and direct consequence of school instruction. The larger part of our behavior, however, is not the result of formal education. Rather, it is the outgrowth of things we have experienced. What we are, what we believe, and what we do are all inextricably interwoven with what we have encountered in our past. It is for this reason that the world contains so many contented dishwashers and discontented bankers. It may be, therefore, that where coping ability is at stake, for many children the lessons of feeling will offer more profit than the lessons of intellect. Experience, in short, may not teach the best lessons, but it unquestionably is the most powerful teacher. "Who speaks of victory?" wrote Rilke, answering that "Survival is all." How many of us, like Rilke, strive desperately merely to survive the vagaries of our lives.

The implications to be drawn are self-evident. Not only must the school provide successful experiences, it must also offer corrective ones that countervail earlier trauma in the individual's past. This is not to suggest, let me be clear, that education take the shape of therapy, as we ordinarily define the word; it is to suggest, instead, that by analyzing the nature of the child we can obtain useful clues as to the kind of education he most needs, and thereby create a curriculum that is, among other things, a therapeutic experience.

The ability to cope—to reaffirm the critical target of schooling—requires that the student train his powers of reason and that he acquire a firm base of knowledge with which to reason. Lest this reasoning be clouded by distortion and misperception, however, it requires also that the student form a healthy set of emotions. From these three—an uncrippled personality, a reservoir of useful knowledge, and a disciplined mind—come the secondary skills of coping. The child's talents are set free so that he may engage in activities that sharpen his ability to identify and solve problems, to think through and choose an organization of values by which to live, to develop a sense of social consciousness, to master some form of expertness that ultimately can be translated into a vocation, and—of growing importance as material abundance becomes increasingly less problematic—to muster an interest in altruism and a desire to serve the public good.

Education invariably is a compromise between the learner's capacities and the curriculum. Programs of instruction are engineered according to group norms and aimed toward the common requirements of the mass rather than the special needs of the individual. In times past, there was little escape from such organization by convenience, for economic realities made individualization prohibitive. However, this is no longer the case. Money has not suddenly become available in rich abundance, but contemporary technology, amid all the difficulties it provokes, has now made a new approach to individualization possible.

It is this possibility that gives rise to our third postulation: the school must concern itself with the uncommon educational necessities of each child, with the particular social, emotional, and intellectual needs that stand between the person and matriculation to successful adulthood.

The ineluctable fact is that any given curriculum, howsoever good, will be appropriate for some children and inappropriate for others. The great flaw in our present endeavors may lie in our hopeless search for universal solutions, for a course of study that will fit everyone. In the existing system, for example, to satisfy what we take to be the requirements of the majority, we must ignore the learning needs of various minorities and, for these youngsters, school becomes a losing proposition. Chicano children, who hear only Spanish spoken in their homes, frequently are assigned to classes for the mentally retarded because they do not do well on intelligence tests that are given in English. In short, the typical middle-class school cannot adapt to the cultural values of many ethnic minorities without, at the same time, violating the middle-class ethos. Attitudes regarding leisure, industriousness, cleanliness, and diet vary according to social mores. The present construction of the curriculum, however, compels all children to accept the dominant, white point of view. Hence, for many children, the contradictions between home and school create a vast cultural shock, one that may diminish the child permanently. It is hardly surprising, therefore, that the dropout rate among Indian students is more than twice the national average.

The curriculum also fails, on several other counts, to accommodate individual differences among children. As Eisner noted earlier, the nonverbal child is doomed from the start because nonverbal teaching is exceedingly rare. Even for the student who does have the requisite verbal skills, the depersonalization of learning erects still other impediments. It is tragic testimony to our curricular shortsightedness that children may still fail in school because they have little inclination to memorize, say, the dates of the Roman wars. We seem, somehow, to have forgotten that it is continually necessary to readjust the curriculum to the society. Much of the schools' current instruction was designed, in theory and practice, to solve the requirements of an earlier age. It is hard to fault students, consequently, who view compulsory education as an uncompromising indoctrination into a world that is largely gone. For the high school senior, seeking desperately to find a semblance of order and direction to his future, the dates of ancient wars are strangely incongruent.

As Bloom reminded us in a previous chapter, many students apparently fail merely because they are not impelled by sufficient motivation. There is nothing wrong, after all, in knowing the dates of an old military battle. It is conceivable, in fact, that a student—pursuing an intellectual problem of personal interest—might find the information interesting and useful. But it is this essential linkage between individual interest and man's accumulated warehouse of information that so often is overlooked. Unless school is meaningful, making sense in the student's own private context, the incentive to learn cannot help but be inadequate; as many teachers are beginning to discover, a good grade on an examination, or a gold seal on a diploma, no longer suffices as a compensation for boredom.

In our way of schooling, individualization has its high point at the inception of the formal educational process, in the early primary grades. Thereafter, it is continuously on the wane. During adolescence, as a consequence, when the student's search for a personal identity is most pressing, he receives the minimal degree of individual attention. For such students, already caught in the tribulations of insecurity, an unreal school is almost unbearable. They are beset, like many of their elders, with a pervasive feeling that life should offer more than they have yet found. Loneliness, self-doubt, restlessness, and uncertainty follow upon one another in a stream of periodic malaise.

As the work of Kenneth Kenniston has shown, "What characterizes a growing minority of post-adolescents today is that they have not settled the questions whose answers once defined adulthood: questions of relationship to the existing society, questions of location, questions of social role and life-style."[2] In a time of accelerated social change, youth

2. Kenneth Kenniston, "Youth: A New Stage of Life," *The American Scholar,* Autumn 1970.

creates its own psychopathology. As the societal scene and the conditions of life alter, people adjust accordingly. The young, unencumbered by a longer personal history, have fewer adjustments to make, more readily accept newer attitudes and values, and thus are out of step with the older population. This separation, however, takes its toll in unsureness. Young people, therefore, frequently seek to postpone adulthood—that is, to delay in making those decisions that commit one to values and behavior that must largely be sustained throughout adulthood. Because they already suffer from feelings of depersonalization, schooling that is bereft of an opportunity to develop a sense of self becomes a kind of psychic prison.

Reduced to its essence, this last of the three postulations centers on the question of our ethical right to perpetuate a curriculum that may contradict the child's interests and life-style, which frequently mandates methods that do not fit his nature, which demands allegiance to selected bits of knowledge that, in the long run of life, probably are inconsequential, and which do not facilitate his search for meaning and personal identity. Succumbing to the hypocrisies of convention, we seem to have demanded in too many instances that the child adjust himself to the mechanics of the school and, correspondingly, displayed a remarkable unwillingness to adjust the school to the child. The reasons for this rigidity, when the evidence is put to hard test, rest in the convenience of the old and in the false worship of tradition.

The need for change, to return to the opening theme, is thus great. The ideas that I have summarized here, outlining the dimensions of the necessary reform, are hardly new. Some, in fact, were born in centuries past. What is new, however, is the ripeness of the time, the possibility that the ideas first came to light before the world was ready for them, and that their moment has now come.

Just as men must sometimes act before they know what is right, they sometimes know what is right before they are able to act. The turn of the tide brings conditions that are particularly favorable and it may well be that the propitious time is now at hand. We have begun to realize, for example, that technological development, yielding both new solutions to old problems and new problems, will always occur at an increasing rather than decreasing rate. And we have begun to realize, as well, that institutions such as government, church, and school change only when their weaknesses become so obvious that a dissatisfied constituency imposes undeflectable demands. In the face of the violence, the disease, the drug epidemics, and the alienation that have recently characterized youth in America, the public may have reached the point where it is willing to reexamine the purposes of education and the methods by which successful humans are best produced. Should this be the case, there is hope for change and for a better kind of curriculum.

10.

A reform must have its blueprint if only to establish a point of departure and a plan to be altered. Nine changes, ranging from the creation of a more hospitable environment to the invention of new kinds of schools, would seem to be in order.

chapter 10

A CURRICULUM STRATEGY FOR THE FUTURE

.

Louis J. Rubin

THE NATURE of the reform that is needed begins to take shape. If the arguments in the previous chapters have merit (and most are hard to refute), the future clearly will demand a new kind of school. The required changes, to be sure, are difficult, but they are far from impossible. What is of greatest importance is that we overcome our fear of the unknown, recognizing that the benefits to be gained will more than compensate for the inevitable stresses of the transition.

What, then, can be said about the reform we need? Taken collectively, the points of view expressed throughout the volume indicate nine essential changes.

DEVELOPMENTAL NEEDS

First, we must shift the basis of the curriculum from an arbitrary selection of subject matter to that which is of immediate importance to the child's development. At present, only token gestures are made toward the learner's psychological health; in the main, schools give dominant attention to scores on academic achievement tests. Most people seem to subscribe to the notion that cognitive learning is worth whatever price it costs. We seem, in fact, to be more than willing to settle for knowledgeable neurotics. This bias stems not so much from the misconceptions of school authorities as from the preferences of the public itself. In short, the adult society has not yet grasped either the distinction between knowledge and wisdom, or the necessary balance that must exist among sound values, emotional security, and an informed mind.

Designing a curriculum that is responsive to the learner's endlessly changing requirements will necessitate not only a greater emphasis upon individualization, but a willingness to restructure the ends and means of instruction, and to place a much larger reliance upon both technology and the available learning experiences in the outside community. As Bloom has shown, we now command the necessary theory and machinery to virtually guarantee whatever cognitive accomplishment we consider sufficiently important. It is not too farfetched to assume, moreover, that similar guarantees could be made with respect to aspects of social adjustment. The critical need is to devise an efficient method for diagnosing the student's developmental needs on a multilateral front. We must be able to determine, in other words, not only how well he can read and count, but how he reacts to his social milieu and how he feels about himself. Such diagnostic devices are well within our reach and it is insufficiency of desire rather than incompetence that has kept us back. This is not to imply that schooling should be a matter of remediating observed and presumed defects in the child. A supportive environment, allowing natural growth to occur, is of course indispensable. But without some sort of diagnosis, we cannot determine the particular kinds of support the child most requires.

The needs of the young vary not only among children but, from time to time, within the same child. The educational system must therefore have a corresponding flexibility. An emotional crisis may erupt and pass, a deficient knowledge of grammar may handicap the student's ability to express himself, and the disappearance of a treasured possession may pose a problem in values; these matters must be dealt with, as the opportunity arises. The predetermined course of instruction, therefore, ought to serve as a superstructure, defining essential objectives without obstructing the other elements of personal growth that are associated with the subject matter at hand.

In such a flexible curriculum, instructional priorities are set not by society's conventions but by the child's own requirements and concerns. And, in such a curriculum, artistry in teaching is more dependent upon perceptivity than didactic finesse. In the learning process, it is the teacher's subtlety of insight and sensitivity to the clues the child imparts that provide the basis for astute diagnosis. There is currently no substitute for delicate judgment and a finely honed skill in reading behavioral signs correctly. Once the true nature of the problem has been ascertained, the corrective experiences can be selected and initiated.

Short of this kind of curriculum, it is impossible to avoid the debilitating by-products of a mass system designed to serve the public. For so long as we conceive of children as a social herd, failing to recognize the individual in the group, we cannot help but perpetuate the tragedies that occur when some learners fail to meet goals that are impossible for their stage of development, while others are alienated through wasting their energies on things they already know.

FACTS AND FEELINGS

Second, we must seek to deal with feelings as well as facts, fashioning a curriculum that provides a better balance between cognition and affect. As Jones points out in a preceding chapter, we now run the risk of replacing our long-standing prejudice in favor of cognitive learning—which denied the place of emotion in the educational process—with an equally deficient preoccupation with pure affect. We may thus again miss the point. It is, as Piaget suggests, the interchange between the two—their essential reciprocity—that must be considered the bench mark of a good curriculum and quality instruction. What we most require is a teaching methodology that enables us both to use subject matter to clarify feeling and emotion and, conversely, to use feeling and emotion in making the subject matter more meaningful. Neither, by itself, suffices as true education.

We are in the midst of an era of intense concern with the quality of life. People today are a good deal more intrigued with their inner lives than once was the case. When existence was harder, the range of acceptable behavior narrower, and the willingness to postpone gratification stronger, we were somewhat less preoccupied with our emotional well-being. It is therefore not surprising that an unwarranted mysticism has evolved with respect to the nature of affect and psychological health.

Our emotions are triggered by the way we perceive and assess a situation. If the assessment is gratifying, our emotional response is pleasant. If, on the other hand, the assessment leaves us dissatisfied or threatened, anxiety increases and we are beset with unpleasant emotions. We then respond with behavior prompted by these emotions. It is thus clear that both our experiences and our actions are heavily influenced by our feelings. Hence, a child's emotions may either enhance or impede his learning success.

One might suspect, as a result of all this, that a school free of anxiety, stress, and tension is the ideal toward which we should strive. But the world, unhappily, does not so work. For most of us, feelings of fear, anxiety, frustration, and stress are inevitable. As we go about the normal run of our affairs, there is little possibility of preventing the brain's limbic system from stimulating, upon occasion, a vast array of unpleasant and uncomfortable emotion. Whenever and wherever we find our circumstances threatening, bad feelings are unavoidable.

Because this is so, to place the child in a school free of anxiety and stress would be to do him a lasting disservice. For only through controlled exposure to emotional tension and frustration can the child learn the crucial skills for their management. Learning to cope, in short, is learning to respond to one's destructive emotions constructively. This is not to say, let me be clear, that there is merit to stress that is not converted into a learning episode, or that an accumulation of excessive stress does not create permanent trauma. People subjected to deep-seated fear in childhood remain forever fearful of similar situations. But as Jones suggested on an earlier page, it is not stress, but *unregulated* stress, that plays havoc.

Through cognitive insight our emotions become more understandable; and through understanding, they become more manageable. The interaction between affect and cognition—the counterpoint they weave—is therefore made clear. As events occur in our lives we assess their probable impact on us. Depending on the nature of this assessment, we react with feelings of joy, disgust, terror, and so on. Where the emotions are involved, one man's cup of tea is indeed another man's poison, for in the assessment of a situation, one person will find cause for elation and another for despair. A school assignment calling for an oral report in front of the class will fill some children with excitement and others with apprehension. The attending flow of emotion unleashes a string of visceral reactions and an impulse to act in one way or another. How one chooses to act—the devices through which one copes—therefore becomes the question of essence. How, in other words, do we best deal with emotional turmoil?

Consider, for example, the situation of a high school history student. The teacher routinely makes long assignments on factual matter that the student finds boring and meaningless. The student would be heavily inclined to skip the assignments but his grade is important both because he wishes to enter a good college and because of parental pressure. He is locked, consequently, in a conflict that generates feelings of frustration and anger. What, then, are his coping alternatives?

Seemingly, the easiest solution would be to accept his plight, grit his teeth, and stoically carry out the assignments. The external problem would thus be resolved, but the inner conflict and the feelings of anger and frustration could well remain. Compelled to accept authoritarian dictate, to spend his time in ways he regards as senseless, the student despises himself for lacking the courage to uphold his convictions and despises, as well, the system that imprisons his sense of autonomy and self-direction.

An alternate coping device would be to modify his

own pattern of attitudes and values. Perceiving that the conflict was inevitable, for example, he might decide that the emotional discomfort was too great a price to pay, and elect, instead, to alter his point of view. He might persuade himself, illustratively, that a knowledge of history might someday be useful, and that, by budgeting his time carefully, he could accomplish the assignments with minimal self-denial. Here again, the external problem is resolved and the internal conflicts are at least partially reduced. Psychological accommodations of this sort have great functional value, particularly when the anticipated rewards have sufficient appeal. Yet, the conditions that spawned the conflict remain, and in a moral sense the solution is less than ideal.

Still another option, however, is open to the student. He might choose to remain captain of his own soul, to retain his autonomy, and to respect his own convictions. He might conclude, in brief, that a good grade was mere pottage in contrast to his own beliefs, and therefore elect to drop the class. Assimilative behavior of this sort, in which one adjusts to the social scene on one's own terms, rejecting society's bribes, conventional values, and the security of acceptable behavior, offers, as its greatest prize, self-respect and the ownership of dignity.

Because such alternatives exist, there must indeed be a place for affective considerations in a cognitive curriculum. Children *can* learn through school experience to cope with their feelings and to manage their emotions. To flesh out this curriculum, permitting the widest possible interplay between knowledge of self and knowledge of world, we must consciously seek to flush forth the personal feeling evoked by subject matter and, in turn, to use subject matter that clarifies and illuminates the student's personal emotions. Which is to say that teachers must build their practice around two questions that have almost infinite power to deepen the learner's insights: what are the facts surrounding one's feelings, and, what are one's feelings regarding the facts?

The body of the emerging curriculum must have dual dimensions. Its skeleton is a structural synthesis of the knowledge produced by scholars and scientists; its heart is the application of this knowledge to the challenges of living. The old body is not being abandoned; it is being fattened, splinted, renovated, and revitalized. The new curriculum is deliberately anthropocentric rather than centered around either cognition or affect. It employs heuristic processes that involve the child, which make him do the work and receive the prufit, and which engrave the experience (and the process by which it becomes an experience) upon his personality.

INNER STRENGTHS

Third, as we attempt to improve the child's emotional response to his world, we must seek to build his inner strengths. Here, too, the school must probe new curricular ground, searching out and testing teaching techniques that make the lofty ideal of personal growth somewhat more of a reality. Inner strengths embody both a resilience to life, a rebound capability that enables one to survive temporary failure, and such ancient virtues as perseverance and stamina. Moreover, because few of us are free from unconscious conflicts, inner strength also implies a willingness to tolerate frustration and the desire to conquer what we have come to call our psychological hang-ups.

The attributes of inner strength are learned and

they therefore can be cultivated through direct experiences, through cognitive insights, and through other activities that lead to a better understanding of one's emotional predispositions. Perseverance and stamina, for example, are largely attitudes of mind, and teachers so inclined can do much to reinforce children at that point when quitting is most seductive. Similarly, when there is a deliberate attempt to draw out the child's emotional reaction to an intellectual idea, great benefits accrue: the idea itself will likely take on deeper meaning, the child is made more aware of his own nature, and a base is thus established for authentic growth. This stratagem, I believe, results in the strongest and most powerful linkage between a subject, the learner's self-concept, and his sense of relevance.

An effort to build inner strength will also lead to a surer sense of self. In Abraham Maslow's elegant phrase, there is in every human "a real self to be discovered and actualized." It may be that by extending the ego development of children, the young can heavily influence the kind of people they will become, almost to the extent of inventing themselves. McClelland's work in achievement motivation, for example, seems to have demonstrated that by consciously shaping their own psychological motives, people can alter the formation of their personalities. Using Erik Erikson's conceptions as a point of departure, McClelland devised training procedures that cause people to adopt more mature motives. The method, somewhat oversimplified, involves the use of instructional activities that make people more aware of the images associated with achievement and success. A typical device consists of allowing children to set goals that carry moderate risks for themselves, and reinforced by support and feedback, to reach accomplishments that are personally satisfying and rewarding. Presumably, other facets of the human personality should also lend themselves to such manipulation, thereby affording another piece of connective tissue between affect and cognition.

Much has been made in recent time of the identity crisis—of the individual's inability to recognize his own special character, his difficulty in attaching meaning to life, and his ubiquitous lack of direction. It has been widely assumed, in this regard, that there is a real self to be uncovered. It perhaps makes equal sense, however, to think of personal identity as something to be built, slowly, through trial and error, over the course of one's educational life. The raw materials of identity—values, attitudes, beliefs, and a sense of what is important and trivial in life—are rooted not only in self-awareness but in history, aesthetics, and other disciplines of the mind. This is not to say, lest I be misunderstood, that questions of value can be entirely settled by a classical education; it is to say, rather, that information and reasoning are essential elements in the formula for acquiring a set of beliefs about what the good life ought to be. If this reasoning is correct, there is still a further advantage to be gained by using the curriculum to shore up the student's inner strengths.

The most compelling reason of all, however, lies in the fundamental proposition that people can be different from the way they now are. Given sufficient courage, incentive, and will—inner strength—children can learn to alter their behavior, bringing it more in accord with their visions of the kinds of persons they would like to be. Learning how to identify this behavior, and how to most effectively bring it about, must surely be among the most important, if not the pivotal, lessons in the curriculum.

Although there is an accumulating body of theory, we do not yet have a workable set of teaching methods for dealing with these objectives. The humanistic education movement that has recently ascended to prominence is aimed at the stimulation of the imagination, the exploration of fantasy life, and the expression of emotional feeling. The teaching devices normally involve improvisations, dance movements, games, and a variety of nonverbal exercises. Whatever their other virtues, however, they fall short of a solid integration of facts and feelings, and educational research and development are thus faced with some unfinished business.

The importance of reliable teaching techniques is difficult to exaggerate. The education of the emotions and the fabrication of inner strength are perhaps the most demanding of all teaching tasks. They call not for therapy but for skillful pedagogy; for organization and structure, not unconstrained free play. The child's freedom to follow his own imagination and to play out his own creativity are classroom imperatives, but these can flourish within a flexible structure. Indeed, without reasonable rules and constraints, the exercise of creative imagination is unreal, for all human achievement must occur inside the framework of the conditions that prevail. There is, in short, a great deal more to teaching than merely getting out of the child's way.

NATURAL LEARNING

Fourth, we must look anew for content of greater significance, for learning experiences that have a stronger connection with the child's external world, and for educational processes that integrate knowledge, feeling, and behavior.

The idea of natural learning is scarcely new. We have tended to avoid such instruction for the simple, but sufficient, reason that artificial learning experiences are more easily managed. Convenience and orthodoxy are the real enemies.

Natural learning does not necessitate antiintellectualism; it need not impede solid cognitive accomplishment; and it should not abridge the teacher's responsibility for leadership. Natural learning, instead, means that because there are options through which an affective or cognitive goal can be attacked, that, wherever possible, the instructional task should involve a pursuit of genuine interest to the student, and that it fit his natural style of learning. Which is to say that the student ought to understand the point of an assignment, and have some part in determining how it is to be accomplished. Thus, if we wish the student to grasp the significance of war, we must allow him to choose from a variety of worthwhile activities that yield the desired understanding, and we must convince him of the advantages to be derived from such understanding. He may prefer, for example, to study Vietnam rather than the Civil War, and he may be more interested in military weaponry than in battle dates. As man's storehouse of knowledge expands, selection rather than saturation must be the hallmark of good curriculum.

Moreover, there is no real reason why some curricular routes cannot lead to the child's out-of-school involvements. Children watch television, talk with their parents, attend movies, rodeos, and baseball games; they build model airplanes, chase butterflies, and build tree houses; they quarrel with their friends and suffer intolerably when they do not receive an invitation to a prized birthday party; they wonder why stars shine and the moon disappears; and, not infrequently, they know a vast amount about subjects that are never taught in school. As they live their lives, children think, feel, sense, dream, and fantasize. They do not, however, in their psychic eye, compartmentalize the learning events of their environment. School may be a place where one must remain silent, and an empty lot a place where one can "do one's own thing," but, all in all, it is the totality rather than the fragments of our cumulative experiences that affect our development.

With a more elastic curriculum, one that took into account the learnings that occur in homes, on street corners, and elsewhere, our conception of the educational process could expand greatly. We tend to forget, for example, that while psychology, sociology, political science, and anthropology are not usually taught in the elementary school curriculum, many of their significant principles can easily be related to children's out-of-school concerns. Beyond this, relevance is a two-way street; the procedure can be reversed, taking children's out-of-school interests into the formal curriculum. How much might a boy interested in ecology learn from a systematic analysis of pollution levels in local streams, for example; or what amount of learning excitement might be kindled if a girl interested in clothes could compare the dress costumes of various primitive tribes? I have argued, elsewhere, the case for process as content,[1] suggesting that inasmuch as any cognitive learning goal could be learned through a number of different intellectual processes, some of greater worth than others, the choice of a particular process was itself an important curricular decision. The same argument, I be-

1. J. Cecil Parker and Louis J. Rubin, *Process As Content* (New York: Rand McNally, 1966).

lieve, is equally germane here: the availability of different options affords us the possibility of increasing the naturalness of the learning situation by catering to the student's intellectual appetite. Indeed, it is this ability to make seemingly irrelevant ideas fit the child's own concerns that separates the mediocre and the gifted teacher.

THE TAILORING OF INSTRUCTION

Fifth, we must begin to invent a repertory of instructional procedures that make it possible for children of different bents to achieve the same educational gains. Throughout most of education's history, we have sought to discover the best way to do something, and attempted to train all teachers accordingly. Little attention was given to the invention of optional procedures for accomplishing the same educational goal. It is now apparent, however, that our inability to achieve successful performance in every child is caused, chiefly, by our limited repertory of teaching materials and techniques: no method will work equally well with every child, or be used with equal effectiveness by every teacher.

Apart from the fact that students tend to have idiosyncratic learning habits—habits made unique by their personality and history—the intellectual interests of the young vary. Thus, if we take the trouble to increase the variety of learning alternatives, we are very likely to improve the achievement of those students who now fail because they do not fit the classroom norm. A larger range of options would also enhance the self-directed learning to which Tyler refers. It may again be observed, in this regard, that the criteria to be used in enriching the curriculum must go beyond mere quantity: the extension must result in an authentic range of choice; the choices must reflect both the cognitive and affective dimensions of personal growth; and the growth must be in the direction of an enlarged coping capability. Wherever these criteria can be met, we will hedge our pedagogical bets to a much greater degree.

As Bloom has made clear, moreover, the needed flexibility must encompass means as well as ends. The teacher who knows but one way to work with a class, or who is master of a single method with which to accomplish an objective, is grossly handicapped. Once more, then, there are powerful imperatives for the continuing professional development of teaching staffs. Teachers must be made familiar with a wider array of learning episodes, they must have greater opportunity to acquire new instructional techniques, and—above all—they must have access to considerable practice in the subtle art of determining which technique should be used with which student, when, and under what conditions.

THE ENVIRONMENT OF SCHOOLING

Sixth, we must alter the environment of the school so that it becomes a more rewarding place in which to be. Nowhere, perhaps, is change more desperately needed than in the social environment the schools create. Why should children hate school? Why should they be victimized by well-intentioned but oppressive authoritarianism? Why should their natural curiosity be blunted by endless boredom? Why shouldn't intellectual play generate learning, and learning generate joy? Our great folly lies in assuming that there is some mystical benefit in forcing children to endure whatever conditions we choose to impose upon them, and in assuming that, because we ourselves suffered as students, so must our young.

Alienation takes its devastating toll in many ways. The resentment bred by meaningless rules, by undue hostility, and by learning that is forced by punitive threat, all diminish the child's faith in the quality of his society. We are too much inclined toward a mindless acceptance of the Tom Sawyer-Huckleberry Finn fiction—we assume that children must naturally resist learning, hate school, and dislike their teachers. Schooling, for most first and second graders, is a delight; for most high school seniors it cannot end too soon. It is in this progressive accumulation of student alienation that the underside of education is most vulnerable.

In the whole of our educational and psychological research, there is nothing to suggest that a pleasant and rewarding environment reduces achievement. Nor is there anything to support the assumptions that drudgery begets wisdom, that failure to learn always warrants a penance, or that boredom is the student's natural lot. The history of education, like that of most other histories, bears testimony to the fact that while institutions change, bad habits remain. Despite centuries of evidence to the contrary, we have continued to worship a flawed notion: one must suffer in order to learn. We seem destined to forever reject the principle that whatever is pleasurable has a powerful lure of its own.

Intellectual rigor, on the other hand, is quite another matter. Discipline, whether imposed inwardly or outwardly, is indispensable. And learning often is hard work. But these constraints need not preclude a pleasing environment or a contented spirit. As Maslow suggests, hard work—when the work has a point —affords a delight and reward in itself. Children are quite willing to apply themselves diligently and to conquer large hurdles when the process is pleasure giving and the accomplishment gratifying. There are, as a consequence, two conclusions to be drawn. Within the educational goals set for our students, the curriculum must be made to have maximum appeal for the individual student, and learning must be made as agreeable as conditions will allow.

What this means is that every child must have the curricular footing that is most conducive to his growth. For one child this necessitates a considerable amount of freedom and for another, close supervision. Some children are happiest working in isolation and others prefer the camaraderie of a group. A new variation of a recurrent theme in the volume—the individuation of learning—thus comes forward once again. All children, alas, do not flourish equally well in the same environment.

Several years back, when I was director of the Center for Coordinated Education on the Santa Barbara campus of the University of California, we carried out an interesting experiment. We were impelled by comments, made in different contexts, by Lee Cronbach and Abraham Maslow. In his presidential address to the American Psychological Association, Cronbach suggested that "natural style" ought to be a significant factor in occupational training. His notion was that—rather than fit the person to the job—it might be more efficient to fit the job to the person. Reasoning from a somewhat different premise, Maslow made essentially the same suggestion in an article published in the *Harvard Review*. Using these ideas as a starting point, we conjectured that it might be possible to match a teacher's style with an instructional method that was particularly appropriate, and going a step beyond, connect both of these with a student who had a high affinity for the same teaching method. We knew that it was possible to devise alternative instructional programs with which to accomplish the same objective, that most children learn more easily with one kind of method than with another, and that teachers usually prefer a particular approach to working with children. We assumed, in short, that it should theoretically be possible to conjoin all three elements in such fashion that maximum congruence was obtained. The experiment was part success and part failure, but it did demonstrate that such "natural fits" are indeed possible, and that when they occur, the gains are substantial.

"Reasoning at every step he treads," William Cowper said, "man yet mistakes his way." As we seek to improve the environment of schooling there is an abiding danger that, confusing cause with effect, we will end up changing the wrong things. It is not, in most instances, the subject matter but the failure to stimulate involvement and meaning that does us in. It is neither predetermined objectives nor unbroken spontaneity that creates problems, but our unwillingness to recognize that each has its time. It is not tests, or even the grades, but reliance on counterfeit motivation that pollutes the learning environment. It is not high standards, but superfluous rigor and false excellence that turn the child away. We must, therefore, become clear about what is what if we are to avoid changes that we do not need. And it is not the degree of formality or informality, but the quality of classroom life, that counts most.

CITIZENSHIP IN AN EVOLVING SOCIETY

Seventh, we must look discerningly at our rapidly changing society and anticipate, as best we can, the knowledge that will be of the most worth in the time ahead. Anticipation, in this context, does not imply speculative futurism. Rather, it refers to the much less risky attempt to predict, from the data now about us, man's coming needs on the near horizon. Schools have always responded to social change long after the fact. This explains, in the main, why curricular history is largely a matter of crisis hopping. Our problems compound, however, because as the rate and scope of change increase, the lag becomes more pronounced and the prospects of catching up more difficult.

It is not by accident that so many of our students develop an intense dislike for the study of history; for the young, the past can only have limited meaning. Elsewhere in the curriculum, as well, we are inclined to labor ancient events in science, in mathematics, in music, and in literature. There is, to be sure, a need to transmit the cultural heritage. On balance, however, we probably overemphasize the past at the expense of the present and future. It is through anticipating what the society will be like when today's students reach adulthood that we can find the best clues for modifying the curriculum. Even if we err in some of our forecasts, we are likely to do the student a greater service than if we retain what is already obsolete. The schools of today are, by far and away, the best in our history. Children receive an education that is greatly superior to that of their parents and grandparents. Nonetheless, we are well behind the times.

It seems certain, for example, that the present generation will have to contend with more leisure than any before it. Yet we have done remarkably little in the way of teaching people to use their free time wisely. Similarly, it is almost incomprehensible that, in the foreign languages, we persist in Spanish,

French, and German—ignoring, as it were, Russian and Chinese, to say nothing of the many tongues of Africa and Asia that are ascending in international importance.

The space age notwithstanding, we do not teach courses in astronomy or oceanography. Nor do we treat technology, geriatrics, or law. These oversights are hardly new; they have been discussed again and again in the professional literature. But this very triteness is tribute to the fact that the curriculum changes with great reluctance and stupifying slowness.

This double fault—of failing both to meet the demands of the present, and to look ahead to the future —is nowhere more apparent than in our anachronistic conception of citizenship education. Pride in country is hardly undesirable, but we seem to have fixed upon patriotism and chauvinism as the essence of civic responsibility. The equally important goals of involvement, altruism, and the desire to participate in the making of a better world, have slipped into the foothills of the subject.

The curriculum floats on the currents of social belief, and the disenchantment of the young adults now in school, I believe, is in great measure the result of a lost sense of personal power and engagement. As a consequence, they tend to look upon themselves not as active participants in a democracy but as helpless spectators to a deteriorating system. Lacking this feeling of potency and commitment, our young have difficulty finding enduring goals; and without these goals there can be neither the impulse to act nor a sense of destination. The circle, unbroken, is a vicious one.

We function, all of us, as both autonomous individuals and members of groups. We are impelled, as individuals, to look after our own ends and to gratify our private desires. But as social beings, we are driven to attend to the welfare of others, to give ourselves, and to serve the common good. These self-serving and other-serving inclinations often compete with one another, and when either is excessively weakened, our peace of mind is somehow diminished. Which of the two dominates, further, is likely to vary according to the social setting in which, at any one time, we find ourselves. Schools provide such settings through their organization, their sanctions, and their standards of conduct. Students tend, in other words, to behave in accordance with the expectations of their groups, because it is the group that fulfills so much of their social needs.

This being the case, it is reasonable to assume that by reconstituting the school setting to make it more responsive to the human desire to function constructively, we can inculcate a higher order of citizenship. In a school of this sort, the student would obtain both intrinsic and extrinsic satisfaction from the use of his talents and energy in serving the community's welfare. And, in such a school, the student would experience worthy citizenship rather than be taught about its characteristics.

VALUE AUTONOMY

Eighth, we must grant our young the right to formulate the values by which they wish to live.

Attitudes, beliefs, and values are branches of the same tree, for all three mold the individual's purpose in life. One's values determine what he considers important and unimportant, what he does, and what he will become. In the cultivation of a successful human being, consequently, the development of a sound value structure is indispensable.

The inculcation of values has traditionally been a prime ingredient in the curriculum. But, as Scriven notes, the approach has largely been one of indoctrination. Put another way, we have sought to transfer the attitudes, beliefs, and values of the dominant subculture to the young. It has therefore been necessary to teach prefabricated values instead of the process of value fabrication.

Ready-made values, however, have their limitations. The individual's right to self-determination aside, some values are made temporal by the ebb and flow of the society. Whereas divorce, for example, was once a disgrace, it now is viewed with reasonable tolerance. Moreover, because the most important values are by-products of our experience, they evolve early in our lives and, once set, are difficult to change. Because they put our world into perspective, establishing order and meaning, we find their reconstruction painful and upsetting, preferring to stick to our ways. For all of these reasons, then, prefabricated values often do not "take." And it is for these same reasons, as well, that value conflicts between generations—and within the same generation—are inevitable.

It is fortuitous on this account that educational researchers have, for the past decade, devoted considerable attention to the problem of value education. Their work has demonstrated that, as children pass through the various stages of ego development, particular kinds of values can be formed. Jane Loevinger, Lawrence Kohlberg, and Jean Piaget, for example, have theorized that these developmental stages take the individual from impulsive behavior to rule obedience, to a self-determined pattern of autonomous morality. Within these theoretical constructs, Lawrence Metcalf, Jerrold Coombs, and

Milton Meux, among others, have hammered out promising instructional techniques. The procedures include teaching devices for the evaluation of evidence, the reduction of differences in belief, and the resolution of attitudinal conflicts. As a result of these and similar efforts, we are now in position to teach the process of valuing with far greater competence than before. The time has come, seemingly, for a revolution in the teaching of values—a revolution that will replace indoctrination with learning experiences that result in the development of an appropriate set of attitudes and beliefs that befit both the time and the person.

These learning experiences must be of different form and shape. Cognitive exercises, like those just described, play a part. But fantasy and feeling also have their place. We cannot observe values directly and must thus depend upon the inclusion of helping experiences. When we fantasize, we imagine a world of our own making. What we fantasize, therefore, is influenced by what we value. Consequently, experiences that lead to a stable framework of belief, to openness, to coping capability, to maturity, and to self-knowledge, are much to be desired. The child must learn to perceive, reason, and choose—to deal with facts—and he must also learn to use his inner sources of knowledge—to deal with feelings.

Perhaps the critical crisis of our time has to do with the conflict between the individual and the society. As separate beings, we cannot do without the benefits the society bestows. These benefits greatly enrich the quality of our existence. Yet we resist, often bitterly, the controls that are exacted in return. Such controls impinge upon our impulses and demand the acceptance of social motives that inherently bring far less satisfaction. Imprisoned by our conflicts, we grow increasingly insecure, lonely, and powerless. We feel helpless before the system, unconsoled by the affluence and luxury it affords. It remains for our values, then—for those attitudes and beliefs that define our goals—to help us find the necessary adjustment. Amid everything else, consequently, the school must endeavor to help its students discover that life, for all of its imperfections, can be worthwhile, and to discover, at the same time, that hard work and morality bring blessings of their own.

A PLURALISTIC SYSTEM

Ninth, because values differ among individuals, we must operate different kinds of schools, designed for different educational purposes.

The schools should serve the people; hence they must be responsive to the various needs and interests that people display. All parents do not value the same kind of education for their children, and the requirements of a particular child can vary enormously from time to time. Upon occasion, freedom, structure, restraint, and independence, all have their virtue. Because the school cannot be all things to all people, a universal educational program will not suffice. We once thought that what was good for one child was equally good for every other; we now know better.

Why must virtually all schools be cast in the same mold, given over to the same basic objectives, and utilize essentially the same methodologies? Variety may be no more than the spice of life, but it is the sum and substance of education. For if we need education at all, it is clear that we need many different kinds. The organization of a school, even a flexible one, is finite, and its possibilities are limited. Hence, at least some of the requirements of its diverse clients must go unfulfilled.

Even when allowances are made for the economic and political factors involved, a healthy range of alternative schools does not present undue difficulty. In a city of, let us say, ten elementary schools, could not different brands of education and different models of learning be made available? Could we not have a school that stressed the classic academic disciplines, or perhaps one that emphasized aesthetics and the arts, another providing great freedom, and still another firm structure, and so on? Given a variety of such options, children could move from school to school as circumstances required. If social adjustment was difficult in one school, another could be tried. If, with a given child, an informal curriculum stimulated insufficient incentive, a shift could be made—temporarily or permanently—to one that was a bit more competitive.

Through all of the comings and goings of the past decade, the fads, the fashions, the innovations, the periods of reformation and renaissance, we have persisted in our search for the ideal school, for a process of education that would fit all. The quest was not without its merits, for although there was some waste, much good was derived. Now, surfeited with an abundance of alternatives, we find it impossible to accommodate them in a single model. What, then, is wrong with satisfying the needs of children in different ways?

These nine changes sketch, if only in rough strokes, the outline of the necessary reform. Their usefulness depends upon the validity of the assumptions on which they are based. Should one choose to reject these assumptions, revisions of quite different character would become necessary. But it seems hard to quibble with the notion that a reform of some sort must transpire.

11
.

Reforms are never pain-less, for they involve the yielding of old ways for new and a realignment of purpose. Remaking the educational order will necessitate a shift in public attitude, a fundamental reorganization of the school, and a different view of the teacher's role.

chapter 11
THE PURSUIT
OF REFORM
•
Louis J. Rubin

WE HAVE CONSIDERED, in the preceding pages, nine potential changes as a means to school reform. These changes, to restate the principal thesis of the last chapter, are as follows:

1. We must shift the basis of the curriculum from an arbitrary selection of subject matter to that which is of immediate importance to the child's development.

2. We must seek to deal with feelings as well as facts, fashioning a curriculum that provides a better balance between cognition and affect.

3. We must seek to build the child's inner strengths as we attempt to improve his emotional response to his world.

4. We must look anew for content of greater significance: for learning experiences that have a stronger connection with the child's external world and for educational processes that integrate knowledge, feeling, and behavior.

5. We must begin to invent a repertory of instruc-

tional procedures that make it possible for children of different bents to achieve the same educational gains.

6. We must alter the environment of the school so that it becomes a more rewarding place in which to be.

7. We must look discerningly at our rapidly changing society and anticipate, as best we can, the knowledge that will be of the most worth in the time ahead.

8. We must grant our young the right to formulate the values by which they wish to live.

9. We must operate different kinds of schools, designed for different educational purposes, allowing individuals to pursue their own special needs and preferences.

The accomplishment of these changes poses a problem of formidable difficulty. Normal resistance to institutional change aside, there exist powerful constraints in the form of conflicting public expectations, the social tensions of the times, dollar limitations, the discomfort inherent in reshaping old patterns, the insecurity attached to taking on new professional roles, and more. In sum, the changes will require three transitions: a realignment of people's attitudes toward the purpose of education, a reorganization of the school's structure, and the development of new work styles for teachers.

Public attitude and expectation exert more of an effect than we might suspect. Schoolmen, recognizing that they are agents of the public's will, tend to respect not only the mainstream of opinion, but what they infer to be conventional taste, as well. Administrators try, as best they can, to find a balance point between the expressed preferences of the vocal few and the unexpressed expectations of the larger body politic. There is, consequently, a peculiar and confounding character to what passes for popular opinion. In most communities, for example, there are outspoken minorities who press for a radical educational program of some sort, a "free school" perhaps, or one in which the learning materials are designed by the students themselves. In these same communities it is likely, however, that the larger majority of parents believe that fundamentals should be given greater emphasis and that discipline should be more stringent. Most educational programs, therefore, are situated somewhere within the range of public tolerance. What the public wants, it gets. Thus, sex education occurs in some school districts but not in others, and, in most instances, the determining force is public preference.

But what is most surprising in this regard is the public's lack of sophistication about the educational process. The average citizen knows remarkably little about the operation of the schools. Parents may know the hour classes end, how well the football team succeeds, the cafeteria menu, and the price of senior class rings, but they are less likely to know why spelling is taught in one way and not another. In point of fact, when most parents think of schooling they think of the classrooms in which they themselves sat long ago.

The consequences of this misunderstanding lie in a mistrust of learning activities that depart from tradition, in a suspicion of methods that are not authoritarian, in a tendency to fault the schools for various social ills, in a gross impatience with innovations that do not yield instant improvements, and in a lack of mutual reinforcement between the teachings of home and school. Under these conditions, when the popular demand for reform reaches its critical mass, the odds are good that often the wrong kinds of changes will be made, as the events of the last forty years have made clear.

Since we have never really attempted to educate the public about education, we know very little about the effect of an informed citizenry on the rate of educational change, on the degree of consumer satisfaction, on the unexplored potential for home-school collaboration, on the possibilities for authentic parent involvement, or on the society's educational values. Nor do we know the extent to which the conflicting lessons, learned in the school and the student's outside milieu, could be resolved.

It seems reasonable to assume, therefore, that a good many of the recommendations that appear in these pages cannot be put to practice without a powerful effort to first familiarize parents with the new kinds of educational goals the changing times have mandated. Bloom's conception of mastery learning, for example, requires us to decide whether we really want to ensure the learning achievement of all youngsters. Similarly, Maslow's approach to personal growth and Jones's devices for dealing with fantasy and imagination cannot be tried unless the public is helped to understand why these things are desirable and why the cost—in time, money, and energy—justifies the benefits they yield. In strange inconsistency, we acknowledge the need to advise the public on health protection, on shifting national policy, on economic progress, and on the development of new military weaponry, but when it comes to the education of those who must carry the society onward we tend to rely, foolishly, on instinct, ignoring the fact that

parents—as the child's first and perhaps most important teachers—have never been helped to know about
the means and ends of their educational choices.

The processes of informing people, of making
them both aware and informed, are indispensable elements in promoting harmonious social change. It was
this conviction—that people must begin to think
about hard educational problems, to talk meaningful-
ly with one another, and to reach greater depths of
understanding—that prompted me to interrupt my
academic interests temporarily and to help establish
a new Communications Coalition for Educational
Change in Washington, D.C.

Established as a non-profit organization and designed to serve the public good, the Coalition draws
its membership from representative educational
agencies, the media industry, and communications
networks whose clients include one or more of education's many publics. Five organizations served as the
initial sponsors: The United States Office of Education, the Corporation for Public Broadcasting, the
Kettering Foundation, the National Education Association, and Curriculum Development Associates,
Inc.

The Coalition has several immediate purposes.
First, it seeks to bring about greater collaboration
among the television, radio, and press media—and in
so doing, to eliminate unnecessary overlap and perpetuate joint enterprises aimed at the common goals
of an educationally informed public. Second, the Coalition attempts to initiate new forms of communications that overcome existing lapses in public
awareness. It is likely that large segments of the population do not now receive—through the communication media they find most convenient—significant information about important educational

issues. By joining the efforts of many separate groups, the Coalition will help to correct these gaps, and coincidentally to assist its members in the pursuit of their own goals with respect to educational change. Third, the Coalition is studying the major education audiences so as to obtain a more accurate picture of their communications needs. Toward this end, the Coalition is investigating:

——The most appropriate medium, or combination of media, which can be used to reach a specified target audience;
——The kind of information each audience wants most;
——The audience's present educational predispositions—its base knowledge, beliefs, and attitudes.

To facilitate these and other studies, the Coalition is working with a number of universities and communications research centers throughout the nation. In all of its endeavors, the Coalition will work cooperatively with the organized profession and the major communication networks.

As the Coalition grows it will perform a number of useful functions. Greater efficacy in communicating educational information will be promoted, and the public's receptivity to desirable change and educational innovations will thus be enhanced. In turn, an informed citizenry will be able to participate more intelligently in the determination of educational policy. I am convinced that such efforts to educate the public about education are prerequisite to any attempt at coherent educational change.

But public education is not enough. The reform will also necessitate a second transition that involves a massive amount of structural reorganization. The revitalization of the curriculum, for example, is crucial. What makes this a task of striking proportions, however, is the sad state of affairs in educational innovation. An incredibly tedious process, changing the curriculum has always required long periods of time because of the need, first, to popularize an idea, then to develop and disseminate materials, and finally, to reorient teachers, parents, and pupils. The changes outlined at the beginning of this chapter, as a case in point, could easily take a decade to accomplish on even a modest scale.

More than simple inertia, however, the reform is impeded by ideological conflict. As Michael B. Katz has made clear,[1] the movement to change education has been complicated by an array of seemingly insurmountable impasses. Community control and integration, for instance, are both desirable, but they are also incompatible. In short, if we increase local autonomy, giving people a greater measure of control over their schools, and a greater opportunity to achieve the educational goals they most value, we have no choice but to allow for the possibility of segregation, ethnicity, and whatever other kinds of radicalism a particular community might want. Such conflicts between the vested interests of particular groups and the national welfare make the political underpinnings of education plain: improvements in the learning of poor children, a more hospitable school environment, greater attention to emotional stability and interpersonal skills—none of these will materialize until they are made congruent with social demand. Thus, although the press for reform must begin with the enlargement of people's understanding

1. Michael B. Katz, "Present Moment in Educational Reform," *Harvard Educational Review*, Vol. 41 #3, August 1971.

and the concomitant realignment of public expectation, it must then move, of necessity, to the required political reorganization. Only when such reorganization has occurred can ideological disputes be resolved and innovation and change proceed in large scale. And only through such reorganization can we begin to do right by those children who now are victimized by an inappropriate education.

The anatomy of the needed reorganization itself has been detailed, to a considerable degree, by the educational shortcomings illuminated throughout the volume. We must take a larger view of the curriculum, concerning ourselves not only with the cognitive aspects of the traditional disciplines, but with the social problems now threatening the society, and with the concerns that are of greatest importance to the learner. We must move away from a rigid sequence of instruction, howsoever skillfully it is fashioned, to a more flexible one that allows the school to accommodate the individual child. We must rearrange the system so that it delivers, at end, a reasonably successful human, able to pursue life without conspicuous handicaps. We must facilitate free access to alternative kinds of education, loosening the bonds of bureaucracy, so that children of different shape are not bent, inexorably, to fit the universal mold. We must use our technology and our theory to diminish, if not eliminate, educational failure, and to neutralize the special learning advantages and disadvantages of social class.

But what of the roadblocks? What barriers stand between the present order of circumstances and the necessary reorganization? The reform cannot begin until our complacency is shattered and people recognize that the alternative to reform is disaster. Worse, even when the weaknesses of the existing system are widely understood, the required corrections are likely to clash with our traditional ideologies regarding independence and self-determinism, breeding fresh outrage, intolerance, and despair. Seemingly, then, there is but one course that meets the test of sanity: the society's educational problems must be made apparent to the citizenry; the plusses and minuses of the available cures must be examined and debated publicly; and the will to accept and act must be summoned.

Currently, the word *accountability* has ascended to high fashion in educational circles. What the term implies, first, is an effort to determine the extent to which learning objectives are achieved; and second, a concentrated effort to reduce failure. Many of our students, for example, do not learn to read adequately. In the same vein, the median arithmetic score of twelfth-grade students, from the largest of our ethnic minorities, is grade six. Determining the cause of these inadequacies is half the battle; invoking the necessary correctives is the other half. The thrust of the reorganization therefore must be directed toward inducing a willingness to expend greater effort wherever it is needed. In the time ahead, we will undoubtedly make great strides im harnessing new technology, in achieving a better symbiosis between human and machine teaching, and in the invention of new and better instructional materials; but these will not eliminate—nor perhaps even reduce—educational failure. Many of our present liabilities can only be overcome by a willingness to make a greater investment in the enterprise—by attempting to make every school as good for its students as humanly possible, by searching relentlessly for higher quality, and by striving both for greater economic efficiency and more economic resources.

More research and development and the expenditures of larger sums of money, in themselves, will not overcome our educational deficiencies. The reading and arithmetic deficits of poor and minority children are not caused by insufficient expenditures or lack of know-how; they are caused by the social deprivation associated with poverty and ghetto life, by the abused spirit that befalls children in these circumstances, and by impotent effort. In this sense, true accountability means caring enough to make a difference: to correct social inequities not only in education but in the antecedent elements of housing, employment, and human welfare.

Finally, it should be noted that the spirit of the reorganization is also of great moment. For goals should not be separated from the ways in which they are undertaken. If, for example, we produce more knowledgeable children and—at the same time—destroy their passion for learning, we shall win a dubious victory. High scores on examinations can be inspired by fear, coercion, bribery, or by the magic of the knowledge itself. Where learning is concerned, then, the inspiration may be of as much consequence as the accomplishment. Those of our students who do well in school, but who resolve, once the diploma is acquired, to never again open a book, have been cheated, in a manner of speaking, out of what is perhaps the best lesson the schools can teach.

Consider, for example, the confusion that now characterizes the efforts to improve the school. Because there has been an excessive reliance on authoritarianism and the spirit-breaking habit of keeping the child in his place, new programs have appeared that seem to eliminate all structure and constraint entirely, substituting a new (and equally bad) orthodoxy for an old. Because we have in the past overlooked the importance of feeling and affect, there is now in many quarters a senseless disdain for academic substance and for the systematic analysis and correction of learning errors. Because competition has been misused, creating destructive trauma for many children, we now witness the emergence of schools in which hard work is ridiculed and the incentive to better oneself virtually nonexistent. Because we have frequently selected subject matter unwisely, burdening the student with meaningless trivia, ignoring his out-of-school concerns, there now abounds a belief that if the child is but happy, the ability to read is extraneous. Where, in the midst of these extremes, is logic and reason?

Clearly, then, the drift of public consciousness—now beginning to polarize toward either a reactionary repressiveness or an unthinking permissiveness—must be set straight. Rather than cater to present public attitude, the reorganization of schooling must have its inception in communications that help parents to perceive the powerful relationship between educational goals and the methods through which they are attacked; and to perceive, as well, the probable benefits and liabilities of the options now available to our mass system of education.

If we do not educate people about education, the impetus for reform will lead to its own self-defeat: we will not get far if we try to stuff unwanted changes down the consumer's throat; we will brook continued hostility and suspicion if we take shelter in bureaucracy and resist the demand for greater community involvement; and children will continue to suffer if, taking the easy way out, we seek merely to gratify uninformed whim.

Beyond the achievement of an informed populace and the subsequent reorganization of the school, there remains the third of the essential transitions—

the evolution of a new kind of teaching role. What this means, in plain terms, is that everything hinges upon the reeducation of the classroom practitioner. Even if the public is made aware of the need for change, helped to examine the options for reform, and impelled to accept and support a new conception of education, the resulting manifesto must be implemented. It has become clear, in the last few years, that superb materials, inspired efforts, rich supporting resources, and visionary ambitions all come to naught in the hands of an unskilled teacher. When all is said and done, it is the encounter between teacher and child that most determines the quality of learning that will take place. Gifted teachers are able to overcome virtually any obstacle that they meet; in the hands of a second-rate teacher, on the other hand, nothing comes to very much. There is, in short, no substitute for teaching competence. As Tyler repeatedly noted, the continuous professional growth of teachers must preoccupy us throughout the foreseeable future.

The able teacher applies with telling effect his knowledge, his skills, and the attitudes and perceptions that order and direct his efforts. Accordingly, it is these attributes that must concern us in the teacher in-service programs that are launched. A knowledgeable teacher, with excellent skills, accomplishes little if his attitudes incline him in the wrong directions. Similarly, the teacher blessed with shrewd perceptivity and a clear conception of educational purpose is doomed to failure if his knowledge is scant or his skills undeveloped. And—as many a university student has come to know—the knowledgeable teacher, striving for lofty goals, can be made impotent by a lack of teaching artistry.

These three, then—the teacher's attitudes, skills,

and knowledge—define the programs of professional growth that must be brought into play. As a start, their true importance must be acknowledged. Next, we must invest our resources in the development of continuing education activities for teachers so that professional competence is sharpened and honed cumulatively throughout the length of a career. Lastly, we must urge school districts to take these programs, and the goals they embrace, with consummate seriousness. Indeed, much that currently passes for teacher in-service education is shoddy stuff, hardly worth the paper on which the offerings are described.

School administrators (and children) have long known that performance ability bears little correlation with training and experience. It is what the teacher can do, not his age or his university credits, that matter most. Moreover, teachers acquire their competence in different ways, building upon their own private talents, but in most instances competence is acquired on-the-job rather than in the training factory. The art, seemingly, is revealed only through practice. It is probable, then, that in-service education is of far greater importance in the making of a teacher than pre-service training.

As with the child, so with the teacher. Reform that is functional depends upon the involvement of teachers, their commitment to different objectives, and their sense of discovery regarding new materials and methods. "Wonders are many," said Sophocles, "and none is more wonderful than man." The teacher who does not experience and pass on this sense of wonder fails his students; likewise, the curriculum that makes tedium out of high drama fails the teacher. Substantive content and intellectual processes involving the use of reason or logic, particularly in the area of affect, must be experienced, understood, and internalized by the teacher. The teacher learns by teaching, but without an engaged spirit and a sense of excitement about the task, bad things rather than good may be learned. And without this same sense of excitement, the teacher may forget—to cite White-head one more time—that "there is only one subject matter for education, and it is life in all of its mani-festations."

These basic characteristics of the teaching art have been known in the past; they are principles of vintage that have retained their vitality and significance. The necessary reform, however, will require new at-tributes, embodying a broader range of knowledge, skill, and attitude. It may well be, for example, that we have ignored, in our training, the most important elements of teaching artistry. The ability to guide rather than instruct; the capacity to be demanding without inflicting psychological damage; an aptitude for continuous negotiation between the cognitive and affective aspects of a lesson; the stability to cope with confrontation; the persistence to ensure learning mas-tery; these and other virtues will be of great essence if the reform materializes.

Not long ago, much was made of the fact that definitive research studies had demonstrated that where the learning achievement of children was con-cerned, the influence of the school was minor com-pared to the influence of the home, and that the im-pact of the teacher was equally minimal. While the research evidence on this score had its validity, we may have misconstrued some of its secondary impli-cations, and perhaps misread the signs as well. Any-one, for example, who has experienced a poor teach-er and a good one clearly knows that teachers make a difference. The difference may not reflect itself in cognitive achievement, but there are other aspects of

life in school that, at least to the child, may be equally if not more important. Good teachers, for instance, do not allow even low-achieving students to
develop a sense of futility and self-hatred.

More to the point, the impotence of the school's
influence should serve as a spur rather than as an ex-
cuse to sustain all that is feckless in the present system. What, in short, could be done to extend the
school's influence? What kinds of experiences would
be authentically compensatory? Could we not mount
programs of teacher professional growth that would
make teachers more sensitive to the children they
teach? Could we not devise ways to assure a better
match in personality between teacher and student?
Could we not put an end to the abuse of the teachers'
dignity, liberating their creative imagination, restor-
ing their autonomy, and freeing them to find personal satisfaction in helping children?

The in-service education of teachers will never
amount to much as long as we remain traitors to our
own wisdom. We cannot expect teachers to survive,
let alone carry, the reform that is needed unless we
provide them with legitimate opportunities to acquire
the prerequisite attitudes, to understand the underlying conceptions and to master the essential skills. If,
for example, there are powerful benefits when children help one another learn, and if we wish teachers
to exploit the potential of such a maneuver, we are
obliged to convince them of its merits, to provide
them with time in which to learn its intricacies, and
to furnish whatever reinforcements are necessary in
the shift from old ways to new.

Knowledge has always been for the sake of man,
his survival, and the grace and joy that make his survival worthwhile. It has been said, aptly, that the
chief distinction between education and training is

that the former increases intellectual options, while the latter reduces them. Knowledge is functional insofar as it permits man to better his present and control his future, neither of which ends are likely to be served by in-service activities that are fragmentary, reducing the art to piecemeal mechanics. The professional growth programs we need must be of a body and not a bone.

Perhaps we ask too much of the reform. Perhaps we cannot expect the public-at-large to worry about our educational infirmities, or expect those who already enjoy the blessings of power to take steps that will relieve the oppression of those who do not. Perhaps the hope that teachers can—through meaningful personal learning and a more salutary work environment—be stimulated to a higher call, is undue optimism. But the realities of our condition being what they are, it would be better to try and fail, than fail to try.

INDEX

•

surviving temporary, 240
threat of, 9
Fantasies, 210, 243
feelings and, 173-192, 255
Fear, 9
Feelings, 5-6
as basis for instruction, 8
behavior and, 12-14, 243
cognition and, 14-26, 171, 236
coping with, 237-239
facts and, 236-240, 261
fantasies and, 173-192, 255
instruction and, 6, 8
intelligence of, 195-214
motivation and, 8-12, 15
primary, 4
Freedom, 10-11, 156-158
Freud, quoted, 174

Gage, Nathan, 53
Gagne, Robert, 169
Generation gap, 13, 72
Getzels, J. W., 181, 192
Glaser, Robert, 128n.
Grading systems, 35, 68, 114-115

Harvard Project Social
Studies, 94
Health services, 33-34, 37
Hero approach, curriculum and, 89-91
Hilgard, E. R., 136
Holt, John, 19, 178, 186
Homes, 37, 46
influence of, 274
and school, 264
Hull, C. L., 150
Huxley, Aldous, 161

Identity, 198, 242
finding of, 160, 162
Identity crisis, 242
Ideologies, 95-99
educational, 215
Illich, Ivan, 19
Imagery, 178, 180, 217
Imagination, 243
Individuality, 9, 12, 95
cult of, 14
Individualization, 228
Inner strengths, development of, 240-243, 261
Innovation, 87-88
Insecurity, 9
Inservice education, *see* Teachers, continuing education of,
Instruction, 4, 22, 35, 50; *see also* Schooling; Teaching

feelings and, 6, 8
function of, 4-5
methods of, 5
quality of, 134-139,
146
tailoring of, 246-247
Intellect, 199, 212-214
Intelligence, 188-189, 193
concepts of, 212-214
of feelings, 195-214
qualitative, 201-204,
207-208
Intelligence tests, 131

Jackson, Philip, 49, 181,
192
Jones, Richard M., 8, 10,
15, 73, 198, 209-210,
237, 264
chapter by, 173-192

Katz, Michael B., 267
Kenniston, Kenneth,
quoted, 228
Kerouac, Jack, 198
Kettering Foundation,
265
Knowledge, 4, 189, 223,
225, 240, 243, 261,
275-276
acquisition of, 5, 10
cognitive, 28
self-, 24, 70-71, 188-
189
Kohl, Herbert, 186

Kohlberg, L., 108, 254
quoted, 105
Kris, Ernst, quoted, 174
Kubie, Lawrence, 175
quoted, 175-176

Laboratories, psycho-
logical, 121
Lahaderne, H. M., 137
Langer, Susanne, 201
Language, 199-200, 251-
252
Learning, 7, 18, 35-36,
58, 217, 224
alternate ways of, 52-
53
from experience, 16,
20
extrinsic, 159, 163
group, 136-137
individual variation in,
122-123
intrinsic, 159
laboratory versus
school, 121-122
level of, 122
mastery, 36, 40, 113-
146
natural, 243-246
nonverbal, 212, 243
potential for, 193
prior learnings as an
aid to, 128
rate of, 122
sequential, 40

286

Thelen, Herbert, 52
Thought, abstract, 15-16
  cognitive, 14
Tomkins, Silvan S.,
  quoted, 4
Transcendentalists, 151
Trauma, 271
Tutors, 135-137, 146
Tyler, Ralph W., 23, 82,
  107, 191, 210, 246,
  272
  chapter by, 33-59
  quoted, 56-57

U. S. Air Force, 43
United States Office of
  Education, 265

Value autonomy, 253-
  256
Values, 13, 25-26, 197,
  217, 253-254, 262
  individual, 256
Verbalism, 193, 200, 212
Verbalization, 182

Watson, J. B., 150
Weiskopf-Joelson, Edith,
  181
Whitehead, Alfred
  North, 210

Youth revolt, 25